rainy day book
of things to
make and do

D0565585

rainy day book of things to make and do

More than 50 creative crafting projects for kids aged 3–10

rps

LONDON NEW YORK

Editor Ellen Parnavelas
Production Laura Grundy
Art director Leslie Harrington
Editorial director Julia Charles

First published in 2012
by Ryland Peters & Small
20–21 Jockey's Fields
London WC1R 4BW
and
519 Broadway, 5th Floor
New York, NY 10012
www.rylandpeters.com

10 9 8 7 6 5 4 3 2 1

Text © Catherine Woram and Claire Youngs,
2010, 2011 and 2012
Design and photographs © Ryland Peters &
Small and CICO Books 2010, 2011 and 2012.

ISBN: 978-1-84975-272-5

A CIP record for this book is available from the
British Library.

Library of Congress Cataloging-in-Publication
Data has been applied for.

Printed and bound in China.

Publisher's Acknowledgments

Ryland Peters & Small would like to thank the
lovely models that appear in this book: Anna,
Blaise, Celia, Charlotte, Emma, Elisha, Honor,
Immy, Izzy, Julian, Lauren, Lily, Maddie, Oliver,
Omar, Peter, Polly, Sean, Tilum, Zain, Aiden,
Alice, Che, Flora, Freya, Harry, Harvey, Honaka,
Keo, Lola, Orla and Rosy.

contents

introduction

What could be better than a fun crafting project to keep children entertained on rainy afternoons? Full of inspiring activities for boys and girls aged 3–10, this book is packed with an exciting range of creative alternatives to endless hours in front of the computer or TV screen.

For children, the experience of creating is every bit as important as the end result. Crafting will fire their imaginations and boost self confidence, as well as helping them learn new skills.

All the classic crafting techniques are covered here, from printing to jewellery-making, sewing, découpage, modelling, stencilling and much more along the way. Every project can be completed using readily available materials, so just follow the step-by-step instructions and you can't go wrong.

Each project is accompanied by a series of simple step-by-step photographs that are easy to follow. You will also find a Techniques section at the back of the book (see pages 152–153) that explains the simple stitches used in the sewing projects, as well as a complete set of Templates (see pages 154–157) to make projects even easier.

Whether it's a fun pirate hat and treasure map for a birthday party, a pretty, appliqué cushion to give as a gift, or a set of froggy book ends to decorate your child's room, this book has something to capture the imagination of every child. After your children have finished all these exciting crafting projects, your family and friends will appreciate being the recipients of many wonderful handmade objects and gifts!

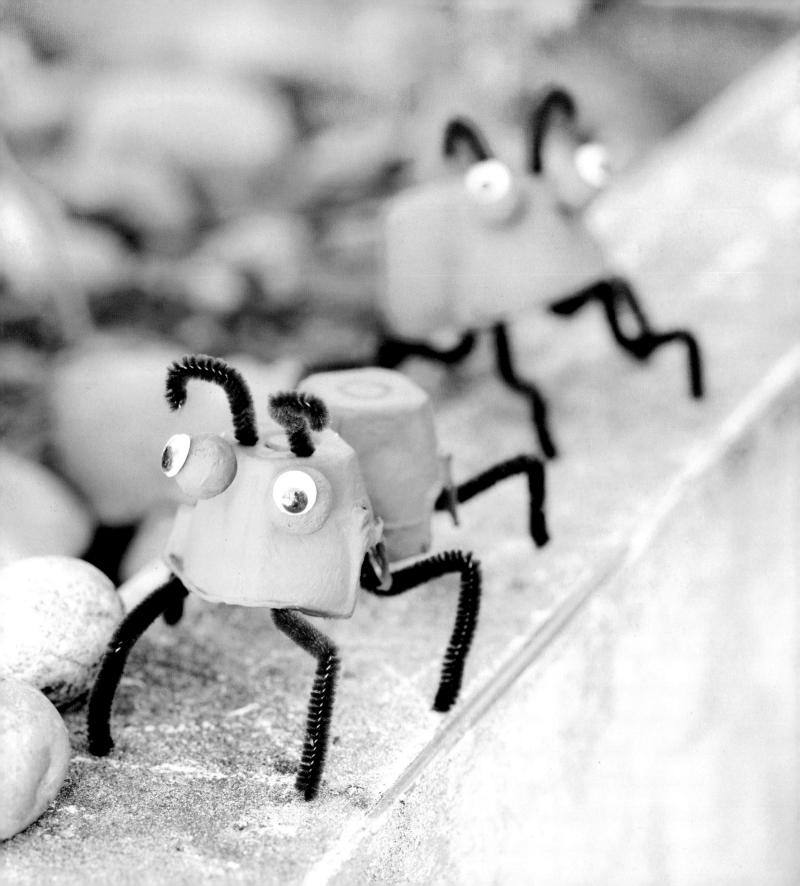

fun and games

paper plate animals

treasure map

pirate hat

travel game

driftwood odd bunch

egg-carton insects

pebble pets

party bag cones

paper plate animals

Paper plates are a versatile addition to any craft cupboard. In particular, they make great masks. This cute lion mask, complete with a furry pompom nose, is just one example.

YOU WILL NEED:
1 paper plate • brown and yellow paint • paintbrushes • saucer for paint • pencil • scissors • strong/tacky glue • small brown pompom for nose • 1 wooden stick 30cm/12in long

paint plate   Apply the yellow paint to the whole plate using a large paintbrush. You may need to apply a second coat of paint for complete coverage. Allow to dry completely.

cut out mane   Use the pencil to draw the triangular shapes for the mane around the edge of the plate. Cut out the triangular shapes carefully using scissors. Draw out the two eyes and cut out using scissors. You may want to ask an adult to cut out the eyes using a craft knife.

apply paint   Use the brown paint to paint the mane, as well as a border of approximately 2.5cm/1in around the edge of the plate. Apply a further coat of paint if required.

finishing   Use a fine paintbrush to paint the lion's muzzle. Once the paint has dried, stick on the lion's 'nose'. Apply a blob of glue to the pompom and stick it in position above the muzzle. Use strong glue to attach the wooden stick to the back of the mask.

YOU WILL NEED:

1 piece paper 50 x 40cm/20 x 16in (we used textured paper but you can use watercolour paper or plain white paper) • tea bag and water • small sponge • paintbrush • coloured paints • fine black pen

tear paper edges Lay the paper flat on a table and tear the edges of the paper to make them slightly ragged and uneven. Repeat on all four edges of the piece of paper.

apply tea stain Leave a tea bag in a bowl of water until it stains the water dark brown. Dip the sponge in the water and squeeze to remove excess water. Dab the sponge all over the paper to stain it. Leave the paper to dry. If the paper dries a paler shade than required, repeat the process.

paint edges of paper Use dark brown paint to carefully paint around the edges of the paper, then leave to dry. This gives the paper a more antique effect. When the edges are dry, you can begin drawing out the island and colouring in your design.

finishing Draw out the island in fine black pen, then use coloured pencils or paint to add palm trees, fish and, of course, the position of the treasure. Don't forget to add the clues. Happy treasure hunting!

treasure map

Create this antique-effect treasure map by ageing paper using tea, water and paint. Draw an island and some clues to guarantee hours of fun spent searching for treasure with friends.

pirate hat

Made from plain black paper, this fun pirate hat is created simply by folding a single piece of paper. Decorate with stamped skull and crossbones motifs.

YOU WILL NEED:
1 piece of A2/16½ x 23⅓in black paper • pencil • PVA/white glue • white or grey card scraps • skull and crossbones rubber stamp • black inkpad

start folding Lay the paper on a flat surface with the short end facing you. Fold the paper over on itself along the long side, like a book. Press flat. Now open the paper out and fold the other way – fold the top down to the bottom edge and press flat.

continue folding Fold the two top corners inward and down to the central line. Press flat using your fingers. You should now be able to see the hat shape.

fold brim Working on the top side of the hat, fold the bottom edge up to meet the bottom of the triangles. Now fold it up once again. Turn over the hat and repeat on the other side. This is the brim. You may want to use a dab of glue or tape on the inside of the brim at each end to hold it in place.

finishing Cut out three circles of paper with a diameter of approximately 7cm/3in. Print the skull and crossbones designs using the rubber stamp and inkpad. Leave to dry completely. Glue the badges to the front of the pirate hat to finish.

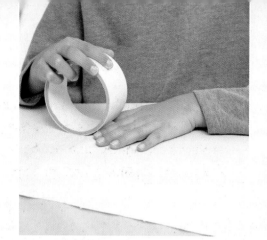

YOU WILL NEED:

45 x 45cm/18 x 18in square calico • masking tape • red fabric paint • stencil brush • pinking shears • paper • pencil • scissors • 1 sheet yellow felt • 1 sheet blue felt • 12 striped buttons (2cm/¾in diameter) • 12 spotted buttons (2cm/¾in diameter) • glue

attach masking tape Stick the first row of masking tape all along the straight edge of the fabric, about 1cm/½in in from the edge. Now stick down another strip of tape parallel with the first one but about 5cm/2in apart. Continue to stick down rows of masking tape until there are four parallel lines of tape in total.

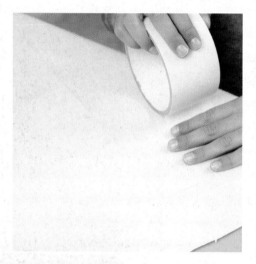

mark out squares Next, stick down rows of masking tape running in the opposite direction at a 90° angle to the original taped rows, leaving 5cm/2in between each row as before. Continue to stick down masking tape until you have created another four parallel lines of masking tape.

start painting Once you have finished sticking down the rows of masking tape, a pattern of squares will be left exposed. Pour some fabric paint into a saucer and dip in the stencil brush. Use a piece of paper to blot any excess paint then paint the exposed squares using a brisk dabbing motion. Leave the paint to dry completely, or it may smudge when you remove the masking tape.

paint squares When the paint is completely dry, peel off the tape. Then carefully stick rows of masking tape over the rows of painted squares, creating another four lines of tape in each direction. A pattern of squares will be left exposed. Use the stencil brush and fabric paint to fill in all the remaining squares.

travel game

This fun draughts/checkers game is ideal for travel as it can be rolled up for easy packing and the felt and button pieces are lightweight too. It's a great project for anyone who loves painting and glueing.

remove tape Once the paint is completely dry, carefully peel off the masking tape. There will be a red and white chequered pattern on the calico. Use pinking shears to trim the edges of the fabric to prevent it from fraying.

make pieces Photocopy the circle template on page 155 and cut it out. Place the template on the yellow felt and draw around it with a pencil. Continue until you have enough pieces. You will need twelve yellow and twelve turquoise circles in total, but you may also wish to make a few spare pieces.

cut out shapes Use scissors to carefully cut out the twenty-four circular shapes from the two different-coloured pieces of felt. Decide which type of button will go on which coloured circle.

finishing Apply glue to the back of each button and press one button firmly to the centre of each felt circle. Allow the glue to dry completely. Keep the rolled-up board and pieces in a drawstring bag, ready for long journeys.

YOU WILL NEED:
pieces of driftwood • glue • acrylic paint in assorted colours • paintbrush • string or rope

select wood   Play around with different bits of wood until you are happy with your arrangement. Glue the pieces of wood together. You may have to hold them in position as the glue dries.

apply base colour   Apply a base coat of white acrylic paint, or another colour, to your design and let dry before adding further colours on top.

paint on details   Use acrylic paints to paint on the eyes and mouth. Use bright colours to paint the body. Sometimes it looks good to leave some of the wood showing.

finishing   You can use any string or rope that you may have found for arms or legs. Glue in position and let dry before you play with your odd bunch creature.

driftwood odd bunch

On walks along the beach keep a look out for bits
of driftwood. Smaller pieces can be put together to
make sculptures. Gather some pieces and when you
get them home, look at each piece of wood, turning
it this way and that. Start placing bits together to make
a figure or animal. Each one will have a character of
its own and be totally unique.

egg-carton insects

Another versatile and inexpensive craft essential, the egg carton can be used to make many items, such as these long-legged ants with their huge eyes and pipe-cleaner legs. You could make a whole army of them and share them with friends!

YOU WILL NEED:
egg carton • scissors • brown paint • paintbrush • 4 brown pipe cleaners • strong/tacky glue • 2 small papier-mâché beads • stick-on eyes

paint egg carton Use scissors to cut out two sections of the egg carton. Paint the carton using brown paint and leave it to dry completely. You may need to apply a second coat of paint for complete coverage.

glue on legs Cut six equal lengths of brown pipe cleaner, each measuring approximately 10cm/4in. Glue three lengths of pipe cleaner along one side of the egg-box carton at equal spaces, then repeat on the other side. Bend the legs to adjust them so that the ant can stand up easily.

stick on eyes Paint the papier-mâché beads the same brown as the ant's body and leave to dry. Glue them to the front of the ant. Now glue a pair of stick-on eyes on top of the papier-mâché beads and allow to dry.

finishing Use an awl or a cocktail stick to pierce two holes just above the eyes. Insert two lengths of pipe cleaner approximately 3cm/1⅛in long. These are the antennae. If necessary, apply a blob of glue to the inside of the head to hold them in place.

cut out features
Cut out a selection of felt feet, arms, and hair in different coloured felt. Look carefully at your pebbles: one may look like a dragon, so you could cut some spines for it; another may look like an alien, so you may want to give it eyes on stalks.

draw on eyes
Using a dark-coloured pen, draw some small circles for eyes on white paper. Cut out the eyes and stick them onto your pet.

attach features
Attach the felt arms, legs, and hair with glue. You may need to hold the felt in place while the glue starts to set.

finishing
Use some scraps of wool to make funky hairstyles. Pipe cleaners in bright colours would also make great arms and legs—you can bend the wire to make hands and feet.

pebble pets

Make these cute pebble pets from rocks or pebbles you can find in the garden, on the beach or in the woods. Look out for ones with holes, they make great ready-made eyes or smiles. Add some arms, legs, or hair and you have an instant, adorable pebble pal.

party bag cones

These card cones with handles are trimmed with dainty braid and make a perfect party bag when filled with yummy sweet treats. You could also make them from black and orange card stock to hold Halloween treats.

YOU WILL NEED:

1 large dinner plate to use as a template • pencil • scissors • 30cm/12in square piece card per cone • stapler • rick rack trim • PVA/white glue • sweets and chocolates to fill

draw out shape Use the plate to draw a semicircle on the piece of card and cut out with scissors. You will need one semicircle of card stock per cone. For each cone, you will also need to cut a handle measuring 2 x 20cm/1 x 8in from the card.

roll into cone Roll the card into a cone shape making sure you hold the pointed end firmly with one hand. Use the stapler to staple the cone together at the top. You may find it easier to do this if an adult holds the cone for you.

glue on trim Measure the top of the cone and cut a piece of rick rack trim to the same length. Apply glue to one side of the trim and stick around the top of the cone approximately 1cm/½in down from the top of the rim. Press down firmly with your fingers and allow the glue to dry.

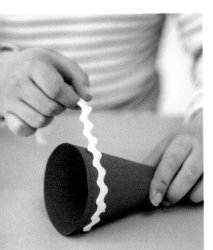

finishing Apply a blob of glue to the top and bottom edges of the handle section. Stick to the inside edge of the cone and press firmly in place. Fill the cones with a selection of candy and small chocolates to finish.

top toys

crazy sock creatures

toy town

dolls' house furniture

finger puppets

cuddly bear

bear's best dress

pebble owl family

YOU WILL NEED:

old sock without any holes
• sewing thread • needle • 3
buttons • contrasting coloured
embroidery thread • polyester
toy stuffing • double knitting
wool for hair • scissors

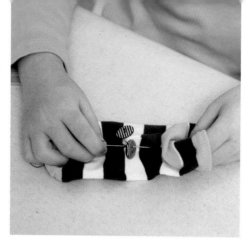

sew on buttons Take the sock
and stitch the first button approximately
2cm/¾in above the heel to form a nose.
For the eyes, sew on two more buttons
about 3cm/1¼in above this and roughly
2cm/¾in apart.

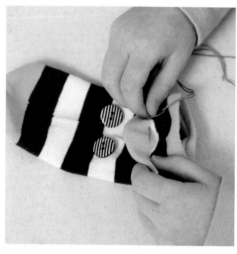

stitch on mouth Use your fingers to fold the heel of the
sock so it forms a mouth shape. Now stitch along the inside edge
of the heel using running stitch (see Techniques, page 153). Use
brightly coloured thread to make a feature of the mouth.

stuff sock Stuff the sock, pushing in small pieces of stuffing at a time. You may need
to use a knitting needle or paintbrush to push the stuffing to the end of the sock. Insert
enough stuffing so the toy is plump and easy to hold. When you have finished, use
whipstitch (see Techniques, page 153) to sew the bottom of the sock closed.

finishing Cut about 20 strands of wool,
each measuring 10cm/4in long, and use
one of the lengths to firmly tie the strands
together in the middle. Now stitch the mop
of hair to the top of the sock toy using
a needle and embroidery thread and
pushing the thread through the knot that
holds the hair together.

crazy sock creatures

Both boys and girls will love these characterful toys made from brightly coloured and boldly patterned old socks. Decorate them with buttons and make their tufty hair from a handful of wool strands.

toy town

Recycle empty juice cartons, cereal boxes and
cardboard tubes by painting them in cheery shades
to create buildings for this cute toy town. Use scraps
of paper in bold hues to make windows and doors
and screwed-up tissue paper for trees.

YOU WILL NEED:

large carton or box (to create basic house) • white paint • paintbrush • scissors • scraps of paper for windows and doors • PVA/white glue • card for roof • sticky/adhesive tape

paint box Using a thick paintbrush, paint the box in your chosen shade. Let the paint dry completely. For the best results, apply a second coat of paint and let it dry.

add door and windows Once the box is dry, cut out squares of paper in contrasting colours to create a door and windows. Glue them in place.

add detail Use a fine paintbrush and contrasting-coloured paint to add the window frames and door decorations. Allow the paint to dry completely.

finishing Cut a piece of card measuring 22cm/9in long by the width of the box. Fold the card 3 times to form a triangle shape and use tape to hold the edges together. Use a paintbrush to paint on the roof tiles. Allow the paint to dry completely before glueing the flat base of the roof to the top of the box to finish.

YOU WILL NEED:
(for the chest of drawers)
4 small empty matchboxes •
glue • 2 different shades of
paint • paintbrush • strong/tacky
glue • 4 small beads for feet •
4 small clear beads for knobs

stick matchboxes together

Apply a layer of glue to the bottom of
the first matchbox and stick to one
of the other matchboxes, pressing down
firmly. Continue sticking until the four
matchboxes are joined together. Allow
the glue to dry completely.

paint matchboxes Paint the outside of the matchboxes
and allow to dry completely. You may need to apply a second
coat of paint for complete coverage.

paint drawers Paint the four drawers using the second shade of paint and
leave to dry completely. Again, you may need to apply a second coat of paint for
complete coverage.

finishing Dab a blob of glue on the
base of each metallic bead and stick
to the base of the matchboxes, pressing
down firmly with your finger until all four
are in place. Now glue a clear bead to
the front of each drawer. You may find it
easier to ask an adult to stick the beads
on for you using a hot glue gun.

dolls' house furniture

This delightful collection of dolls' house furniture is made from recycled matchboxes, cardboard and craft sticks painted in bright colours and decorated with patterned origami papers and beads.

dressing table

Made using eight small matchboxes with a thick cardboard top, this dressing table also features a decorative matching mirror made using a piece of painted card and a mirror cut from kitchen foil.

wardrobe

This freestanding wardrobe was made from a large box of matches. The front of the box was cut in half to create doors. The wardrobe was painted to match the dressing table and has metal feet and bead knobs to finish.

dolls' house bed

A large matchbox was also used to make this dolls' house bed. The headboard is made from large and medium craft sticks painted to match the other furniture. A sheet of prettily patterned origami paper makes a decorative bedcover and pillow.

little tips

Ask your parents to collect different-sized and shaped matchboxes from hotels and bars to keep in your craft box or cupboard. They come in many different shapes and sizes, and the cardboard is often of better quality than standard matchboxes.

YOU WILL NEED:

paper • scissors • 1 sheet felt
• pencil • pinking shears •
needle • embroidery thread •
3-D fabric pen • wooden button
(2cm/¾in diameter) • felt glue •
5cm/2in rick rack trim • felt
scraps • knitting wool

draw template Photocopy the finger puppet template on page 155 and cut it out. Place the template on the back of the felt and draw round it twice with the pencil. Cut out the two shapes using pinking shears.

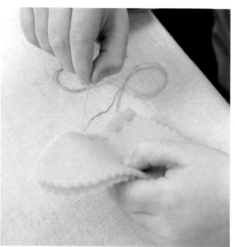

start sewing Thread the needle with embroidery thread and sew the two pieces of felt together using running stitch (see Techniques, page 153) and working approximately 3mm/⅛in in from the edges. Cast off securely to prevent the stitching from coming undone. Now use the 3-D fabric pens to draw a little face on the wooden button, using the two thread holes as eyes. Allow to dry completely.

decorate puppet Glue the button face in place at the top of the finger puppet. Cut a length of rick rack to fit the bottom edge of the puppet and glue it onto the felt. Use the 3-D pen to draw on more hair, buttons and other details as desired.

finishing Cut out a bow-tie shape from a scrap of felt and glue it to the front of the finger puppet to finish. Why not create a whole family of puppets using the same template and add plaits/braids made from knitting wool and other felt accessories?

finger puppets

These cute finger puppets are made from coloured felt and decorated with buttons and scraps of rick rack. The sewing is very simple so this is an ideal project for younger crafters.

cuddly bear

This cute bear is made from a soft wool fabric and sewn together using simple blanket stitch. See the following pages to make a pretty dress for your bear.

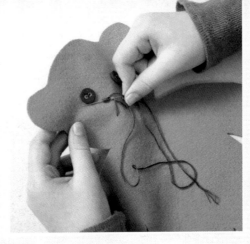

YOU WILL NEED:

paper • scissors • 25 x 60cm/ 10 x 24in wool fabric or felt • pins • needle • embroidery thread in 2 different colours • 4 buttons (about 1cm/½in diameter) • polyester toy stuffing • 40cm/16in ribbon (about 1cm/½in wide)

create template Photocopy the teddy template on page 154 and cut it out. Fold the fabric in half, pin the template to the fabric and carefully cut out around it so you have two teddy shapes. Take one of the body shapes, thread the needle with embroidery thread and stitch the buttons in position as shown on the template. Work the nose in small straight stitches just below the eyes.

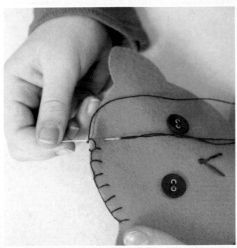

start stitching Thread the needle with the different-coloured embroidery thread. Position the two pieces of fabric with wrong sides together (pin them together if necessary) and begin stitching them together all the way around the edges using blanket stitch (see Techniques, page 152). The stitches should be about 5mm/¼in apart. Remember to leave an opening of approximately 5cm/2in, so you can stuff the bear.

stuff bear Insert the stuffing into the bear through the opening. Take small pieces of stuffing and use the end of a paintbrush or a knitting needle to push them firmly down to the very bottom of the bear's legs and arms. Insert enough stuffing so that the toy is plump and easy to hold but not too firm or overstuffed.

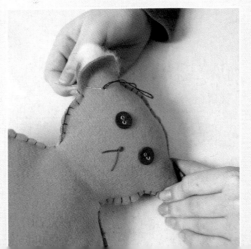

finishing Once the bear is stuffed, sew the opening closed using blanket stitch. Tie the ribbon around the bear's neck and into a bow. Cut the ribbon ends on the diagonal to prevent them from fraying. Sew two more buttons to the front of the bear just below the neck to finish.

YOU WILL NEED:

22 x 36cm/9 x 14in cotton fabric
• scissors • needle • matching
sewing thread • safety pin •
20cm/8in elastic • 25cm/10in
ribbon (1cm/½in wide)

cut out Fold the fabric in half with short end to short end then cut along the fold to give you two rectangles measuring 22 x 18cm/9 x 7in. Place them together with right sides facing and sew along the two long sides of the fabric using running stitch (see Techniques, page 153). Stop approximately 10cm/4in away from one short end to leave space for the armholes.

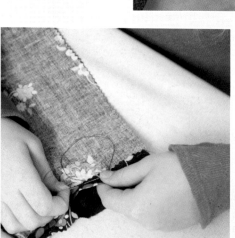

sew sides together You will now have a tube of fabric. At the bottom edge, fold in a 1cm/½in hem and use running stitch to sew it in place. Now, working at the top of the dress where the side seams end, neatly fold the raw edges in 1cm/½in to the wrong side and use running stitch to sew them in place.

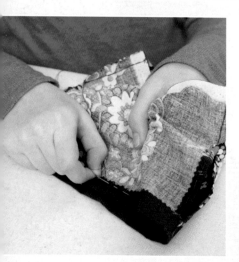

make casing At the top of the dress, fold in a 2cm/¾in hem to the wrong side of the fabric and use running stitch to sew in place. This will form the casing for the elastic, so leave the ends open. Attach the safety pin to one end of the elastic and insert it into one opening. Chase it through the casing and out the other side. Gather the elastic so that it fits the bear's neck, trim the ends and sew them together securely.

finishing Put the dress on the bear and sew together the casing at the shoulders, taking care not to stitch through the elastic at the same time. Tie the ribbon into a bow, trim the ends on the diagonal to prevent them from fraying, and stitch the bow to the front of the dress.

bear's best dress

Make your cuddly bear this simple dress in a pretty floral fabric decorated with a bow.

pebble owl family

This little family of owls is painted with bright, decorative patterns.

YOU WILL NEED:
smooth pebble • white
acrylic paint • paintbrush •
coloured paints or felt-tip
brush pens • varnish

paint base colour Make sure
your pebble is clean and dry. Decide
which side is going to be the front of
the owl and paint it with a base coat
of white. Let dry.

add features Paint or draw on your owl. It is easiest to start
with the eyes. Use lots of bright colours. I have made the eyes in
flower shapes for a retro look.

decorate owl Paint on some wings and decorate with spots, stripes, or flowers.
The brighter the better!

finishing Finally, if you like, you can give
your owl a coat of varnish for extra shine.
Make a few more owls in the same way
and when everything is dry, line them up
on a bedroom shelf to keep watch.

rad room

fleece blanket

twig letters

patchwork cushion

ladybird mobile

bulletin board

découpaged picture frame

froggy bookends

fleece blanket

Decorated with a fun boat motif, this fleece blanket is perfect for cuddling up in for a sleepover! Girls might like to make one from pink fleece, with a flower or heart motif.

YOU WILL NEED:

150cm/5ft fleece fabric
(150cm/5ft) wide • scissors •
boat motif (here it is cut from
printed cotton fabric) • fusible
web • contrastingly coloured
cotton embroidery thread
• double knitting wool
• large needle

cut out fabric Cut along the edges of the fleece fabric to make sure they are straight, and cut off the selvedge. Then cut the corners of the blanket into a gentle curve, which will make it easier when you are stitching the edges.

cut out motif Iron the fusible web to the back of the fabric and leave to cool. Cut out the boat motif, peel off the backing paper and place the motif in one corner of the blanket. Cover the motif with a kitchen towel and ask an adult to help you press it with a hot iron.

stitch motif Thread a needle with the embroidery thread and stitch around the boat motif in blanket stitch (see Techniques, page 152). You may want to add some buttons as extra decoration.

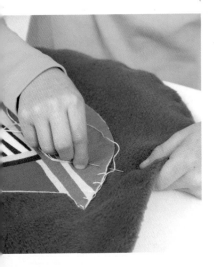

finishing Fold in a 2cm/¾in hem all the way around the blanket and pin it in place ready for stitching. Thread the needle with the knitting wool and work blanket stitch around all four sides of the blanket. The stitches should be about 1–2cm/½–¾in apart.

YOU WILL NEED:
sticks • white paint • paintbrushes • paint in assorted bright colours • glue

select sticks Gather together some sticks of similar thicknesses. Break up the sticks to make different lengths and arrange them into letter shapes. Paint the sticks white. You may need a couple of coats to get a good coverage. Try to keep the different sticks that belong to one letter together.

add stripes When the sticks are dry, paint a series of stripes down some sticks in a different colour. Let dry.

decorate sticks Decorate the sticks further with alternate stripes in a different colour or experiment with another pattern—stars, dots, flowers—the brighter the better!

finishing Glue the sticks together to form the letters. Wait until the glue has completely dried before you display them on the wall.

twig letters

These fun, brightly coloured letters are a brilliant way to personalize your own space and decorate your bedroom.

patchwork cushion

This fun cushion is made from colourful fabric squares. It's a great way of recycling fabric scraps or old clothes you have grown out of. Finished with a pretty flower motif, it adds a touch of style to your room.

YOU WILL NEED:

paper • scissors • pins • assorted fabric squares measuring at least 11 x 11cm/ 4½ x 4½in each • needle • thread • 2 rectangles of fabric, each measuring 40 x 25cm/ 16 x 10in for back • flower motif • small bead • 40 x 40cm/ 16 x 16in square cushion pad

cut out squares On a piece of paper, draw a square measuring 11 x 11cm/4½ x 4½in and cut it out. This is your patchwork template. Pin the square onto the back of the fabric pieces and cut out 16 squares.

stitch together Place two squares together with right sides facing. Pin if necessary. Now stitch the two squares together along one side, using a small running stitch (see Techniques, page 153) and working 5mm/¼in from the raw edges. You could use back stitch (see Techniques, page 153) for a stronger finish, although it will take more time.

clip edges and press When you have sewn together a strip of four patches, trim and notch the seams and ask an adult to help you press them flat using a hot iron. Put this strip to one side. Continue sewing patches together with right sides facing until you have four strips of four patches each.

continue sewing Place two strips together with right sides facing. Pin if necessary. Stitch together along one long side of each strip using running stitch, 5mm/¼in from the edges. Repeat until all four strips have been attached and you have a piece of patchwork with 16 squares in total. Ask an adult to help you press the seams with an iron.

cut out backing fabric From the backing fabric, cut two rectangles measuring 40 x 25cm/16 x 10in. Place them together with right sides facing and pin in place if necessary. Working on one long (40cm/16in) edge, stitch in about 5cm/2in from the edge, using back stitch and sewing about 3cm/1¼in from the raw edge. Cast off securely.

stitch backing together Now stitch inwards from the other end of the long edge for about 5cm/2in, again using back stitch. Cast off securely. There will now be a 30cm/12in gap in the middle of your stitching which forms the opening through which to insert the cushion. Open the fabric out and ask an adult to help you press the seam flat using a hot iron.

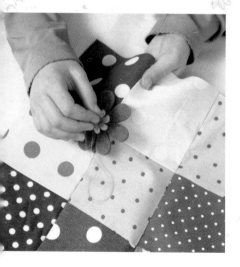

stitch flower Thread the needle and stitch the flower motif to one corner of the cushion front. Sew a bead to the middle of the flower for decoration.

finishing Place the patchwork and back section together with right sides facing. Using back stitch, sew around all four edges, about 1cm/½in from the edge. Turn the cover right side out. Insert the cushion pad and stitch the opening closed using whipstitch (see Techniques, page 153).

ladybird mobile

This cheerful mobile with its bold dotty ladybirds would look great hanging in a window or from a lampshade in a bedroom.

YOU WILL NEED:

paper for template • scissors • pencil • 1 piece A4/letter-sized red card stock • 1 piece A4/letter-sized black card stock • PVA/white glue • nylon thread • red paint • paintbrush • 2 wood battens measuring 1cm x 1cm x 20cm/½in x ½in x 8in • white paint

create template Photocopy the ladybird template on page 156 twice and cut the templates out. Draw around the body template on red card stock and around the face and spot templates on the black card stock. Draw a second set for the other side of the ladybird.

cut out shapes Cut out the ladybird bodies, head and spots. If preferred, you could use black self-adhesive dots for the ladybird spots.

decorate ladybird Glue the face and six spots to one side of the ladybird, as shown. Turn over and repeat on the other side. Repeat these steps to make three more ladybirds. Paint the wooden battens red and ask an adult to drill a hole through the middle of each piece and at each end.

finishing Use a fine paintbrush and white paint to paint on the eyes. Allow to dry completely. Stick the battens together in the shape of a cross, lining up the central holes. Push through a loop of nylon thread to hang the mobile from. Make a hole at the top of each ladybird and use nylon thread to attach a ladybird to each of the four ends of the battens.

YOU WILL NEED:

50 x 70cm/20 x 28in stiff cardboard • 50 x 70cm/20 x 28in sheet of thin foam • star-print cotton fabric 60 x 80cm/ 24 x 32in • pinking shears • 6m/20ft gingham ribbon (1cm/½in wide) • drawing pins • strong glue

cover board Cut a piece of cardboard and a piece of thin foam measuring 50 x 70cm/20 x 28in, cutting the edges on a gentle curve. Place the fabric on a flat surface, wrong side up. Position the foam on top and the board on top of that and trim the edges of the fabric so there is an overlap of about 4cm/1½in all round. Use pinking shears to prevent the edges from fraying.

position ribbons Fold the fabric to the back of the board, pulling it taut so there are no wrinkles. Glue the fabric in place around all four edges. Allow to dry. Take the ribbon and cut four pieces that are long enough to run diagonally across the board at evenly spaced intervals of about 15cm/6in. Repeat, using four more ribbon lengths to cross over the first parallel lines and create a diamond pattern. Allow a margin of about 4cm/1½in at each end of the ribbon so you can glue it to the back of the board.

attach pins Push a drawing pin into the centre of each ribbon cross and press down firmly. Repeat until you have pushed a drawing pin into every ribbon cross.

finishing Turn the board over and pull the ribbon ends to the back. Apply glue to each ribbon end to secure it in position. Allow the glue to dry completely.

bulletin board

This practical bulletin board is made using a piece of stiff cardboard and bright and cheerful star-print cotton. Make one to match the fabrics in your bedroom for extra effect.

découpaged picture frame

Bring the traditional découpage method up to date by decorating a plain frame with simple square and rectangular pieces of bold paper decorated with attractive designs. We finished the frame with rick rack trim and cute buttons.

YOU WILL NEED:

decorative paper in a variety
of designs • scissors • picture
frame with wide edges for
découpage • PVA/white glue •
rick rack trim to fit frame •
buttons to decorate

cut out shapes Cut out a selection of squares and rectangles from the decorative paper and arrange the pieces in piles of the same design to make sticking them easier. You may like to arrange the paper on the frame before you start sticking to work out your design, or you can simply begin sticking and see where you end up!

start sticking Begin sticking the shapes on the frame. Apply glue to the back of each paper square or rectangle. Press the edges of the paper flat with your fingers to make sure they don't curl up. Continue sticking on the shapes until the frame is completely covered.

decorate Apply glue to the back of the buttons and stick them on the frame at regular intervals. You could ask an adult to do this using a hot glue gun, as the glue sticks get very hot.

finishing Cut four lengths of rick rack to fit around the frame aperture. Use PVA/white glue to stick the rick rack to the frame, neatly bordering the aperture. Leave to dry completely. Insert a picture in the frame to finish.

YOU WILL NEED:
one large flat pebble • one thin, wide pebble • two small wide pebbles • paint in assorted colours • small paintbrush • glue • varnish (optional)

paint body Check that your pebbles are clean and dry. Paint some flowers or dots around the larger pebble for the frog's body.

paint head Paint the thin, wide pebble with a base coat of green. Let dry and then paint on a wide smiley mouth in a darker colour.

make eyes To make the eyes, paint a white circle onto the small pebbles and, when dry, add a black dot in the centre of each circle.

finishing Glue the mouth section to the body and then glue the two eyes in position. You may have to hold the pebbles in place while the glue starts to set. If you like, you can give your frog a coat of varnish to give him a nice shine.

froggy bookends

Transform a few pebbles into this happy smiley frog with a little paint and glue. Make two and you have a pair of bookends!

great gifts

bandana notebook

appliqué cushion

doily box

dvd carry case

découpaged tray

silhouette frame

egg cosies

bandana notebook

Use colourful bandana scarves to make these covered notebooks. You can stick pretty embroidered letters to front of the notebook to make the perfect gift for your best friend.

cut out fabric Open the notebook out flat on the wrong side of the bandana. Cut all the way around the book, allowing a 3cm/1¼in margin around all edges. Now close the book and place the spine in the centre of the fabric with the bottom of the book facing towards you. Cut two parallel slits at the top and bottom of the spine. Push these pieces of fabric inside the spine and glue in place. Allow to dry.

start sticking To glue the bandana inside the notebook, place the front cover flat and rest the other part of the book against your body while you work. Neatly fold the fabric to the inside along the long outside edge of the book and glue it in position.

fold corners When the outside edge has dried, fold the corners of the fabric neatly towards the inside of the book then turn in the fabric at the top and bottom edges and glue it in place. Repeat the glueing process at the back of the book and let it dry.

finishing Now stick one or two embroidered letters on the front of the book. Allow the glue to dry completely.

YOU WILL NEED:

paper • scissors • fusible web • pencil • 40 x 80cm/16 x 32in gingham fabric • additional gingham scraps for house and doors/windows • needle • sewing thread • buttons • 30 x 40cm/12 x 16in cushion pad • ribbon • contrast embroidery thread • 40cm/16in ribbon (2cm/¾in wide)

create templates Photocopy the house, roof, window and door templates on page 155 and cut them out. Ask an adult to help you iron the fusible web onto the back of the scraps of gingham fabric, then allow the fabric to cool.

cut out house Place the templates on the paper side of the fusible web, draw around them in pencil and cut out the shapes. From the gingham fabric, cut one rectangle for the cushion front measuring 33 x 43cm/13 x 17in and two rectangles for the cushion back measuring 33 x 24cm/13 x 9½in. Take the larger piece of gingham (the cushion front) and place the house and roof shapes with the windows and doors on top. Lay a kitchen towel over the shapes and ask an adult to help you iron them in place, following the manufacturer's instructions.

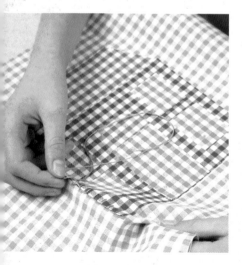

start blanket stitch Leave the fabric to cool down completely. Thread the needle with embroidery thread and begin working blanket stitch (see Techniques, page 152) all around the outlines of the house and roof. Cast off your sewing securely to prevent the stitches coming undone.

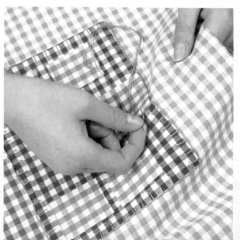

continue stitching Continue to blanket stitch around the door and then the windows. When you have finished sewing, ask an adult to help you iron the stitching on the reverse side of the fabric and then leave it to cool.

appliqué cushion

This cute gingham cushion with its appliquéd house motif worked in blanket stitch would make a great housewarming gift for someone special!

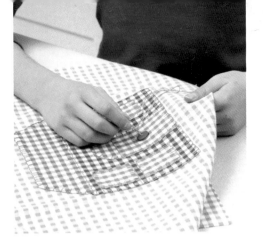

sew on button Place the button in the centre of the door on the front of the cushion and securely stitch in place.

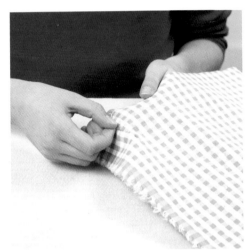

stitch back section Thread the needle with sewing thread. Place the two back sections of the cushion cover with right sides facing and pin in place if necessary. Working on one long edge, stitch in about 5cm/2in from the end, using back stitch and sewing about 3cm/1¼in from the raw edge. Now stitch inwards from the other end for about 5cm/2in, again using back stitch. Cast off securely. There will now be a gap in the middle of your stitching which forms the opening for the cushion pad.

stitch cover together Ask an adult to help you press the seam flat using a hot iron. Now place the front and back sections of the cushion together with right sides facing. Pin in place if necessary. Stitch around the four sides using back stitch (see Techniques, page 153). Notch the corners and turn the cover to the right side.

finishing Cut the ribbon into two 20cm/8in lengths and use whipstitch to attach one end of each piece to each side of the opening at the back of the cushion. These ties will hold the opening closed. Trim the ends of the ribbon on the diagonal to prevent them from fraying.

YOU WILL NEED:

circular lidded box • selection of paper doilies • masking tape • paint • saucer to hold paint • fat paintbrush or stencil brush • paper towel • scissors • PVA/white glue • two lengths of narrow ribbon to fit around the lid • 2 decorative butterflies

stencil lid Place the doily on the box lid in the position to be stencilled. You can use tiny pieces of masking tape to hold the doily securely in place for stencilling. It is important that the doily is not moved during the stencilling process as this will smudge the design. Dip the brush in the paint and remove as much excess paint as possible by wiping the brush on a paper towel.

peel off stencil Once you have covered the whole stencil with paint, allow the paint to dry slightly for a few minutes then carefully peel off the masking tape, if used, and lift the doily stencil off the box lid to reveal the design.

cut out motifs Take a doily and cut out shapes from it using scissors. Different doilies have different designs, so look at them carefully to discover the prettiest shapes to cut out.

finishing Apply glue to the back of the cut-out doily shape and then press it firmly onto the side of the box. Continue sticking the shapes around the box at regular intervals. Stick two lengths of ribbon around the edge of the box lid and press firmly in place and allow to dry. Stick the two decorative butterflies to the lid of the box to finish.

doily box

The delicate lace-like effect of doilies makes
them a perfect craft paper and they can be
cut up and used to decorate many different
objects, including boxes, books and picture
frames. Doilies also make great
stencils with their delicate lacy
shapes, and this plain box
combines both stencilling
and cut-out doily motifs.

dvd carry case

Make this cool DVD carrier for a friend using a ready-made case and decorate it with buttons and stick-on eyes plus a fun skull-and-crossbones motif. This project is great for younger children.

YOU WILL NEED:

fusible web • small piece of fabric with skull-and-crossbones motif • pencil • scissors • round DVD case • 7-8 buttons in assorted designs or poppers • 5 stick-on eyes • PVA/white glue • 15cm/6in rick rack

make motif Ask an adult to help you iron the fusible web to the back of the skull-and-crossbones fabric. Let it cool. Draw a circle on the paper side of the fusible web (a lid would be a good template, or use a compass), making sure that the skull motif is positioned exactly in the middle of the circle.

cut out motif Use scissors to carefully cut out the circular motif. Peel off the backing paper and position the circle in the centre of the DVD case. Ask an adult to help you iron the motif in place, following the manufacturer's instructions, and allow to cool.

stick on buttons Glue your buttons, stick-on eyes and poppers at regular intervals around the edge of the case. Press each button down firmly with your finger to make sure they are securely in place. Allow the glue to dry completely.

finishing Cut a length of rick rack about 15cm/6in long and thread it through the hole of the zipper. Tie the rick rack in a knot and pull the ends firmly to secure. Cut the ends of the rickrack on the diagonal to prevent them from fraying.

YOU WILL NEED:

paper for template • scissors • pencil • decorative paper in a variety of designs • wooden tray • PVA/white glue or glue stick • water-based acrylic varnish • paintbrush

create template Photocopy the diamond-shaped template on page 157 and cut it out using scissors. Place the template on the decorative papers and draw around it using pencil. Repeat until you have enough diamonds to cover the bottom of the tray.

cut out patchwork shapes Use scissors to carefully cut out the diamond shapes. We used origami paper which features decorative patterns, making it perfect for this project.

glue shapes to tray Before you begin sticking the diamond shapes to the tray you may find it useful to lay them out on the tray first to create a pleasing arrangement. Lift each piece of paper individually to apply glue and stick to the tray, so you remember where each shape should go. Use your fingers to press the glued diamonds flat so they are firmly stuck down.

finishing Trim the diamond shapes to fit at the edges of the tray. The easiest way to do this is to lay them on the tray and fold back the edge of paper to the required place, then trim with scissors and glue in place. When the glue is dry, apply one or two coats of water-based acrylic varnish to finish.

découpaged tray

This tray has been découpaged with pretty patterned paper diamond shapes that were glued to the tray then finished with varnish. It's the perfect gift for a grandmother on her birthday.

silhouette frame

The traditional craft of cutting out paper silhouettes is both fun and easy, and they make great gifts for friends and family. Simply photocopy a photograph of your own profile, then cut it out in coloured paper and glue it to a decorative background paper. You can use the same technique to decorate boxes, books and cards.

YOU WILL NEED:

photocopy of photograph of a head in profile • 1 piece of coloured paper • pencil • decorative paper • picture frame • buttons to decorate • PVA/white glue • scissors

cut out silhouette Use scissors to carefully cut out the photocopy of the head in profile. For very intricate areas, you may want to ask an adult to help you by cutting out the silhouette using a sharp craft knife.

draw around silhouette Place the cut-out silhouette template on the back of the coloured paper and use a pencil to carefully draw around the shape. Again, cut out using scissors or ask an adult to help you with a craft knife.

glue to paper Apply glue to the back of the shape. Stick it firmly to the decorative paper and press flat. Allow the glue to dry completely. If required, paint the frame to coordinate with the silhouette and decorative paper that you have chosen.

finishing Decorate the frame by sticking on a selection of pretty buttons with glue or a hot glue gun (a hot glue gun must only be used by an adult). Leave the frame to dry completely. Insert the silhouette and close the back of the photograph frame.

YOU WILL NEED:
paper • scissors • pins • 1 sheet
felt for egg cosy • 1 sheet
contrast felt for flower • needle
• sewing thread • felt glue •
embroidery thread • scissors
• small pompom

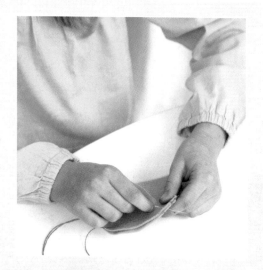

create templates Photocopy the flower and egg cosy templates on page 155 and cut them out. Pin the petal template to the back of the felt and draw round it six times then cut out the six petals. Arrange them in a circle and begin sewing along the inner straight edge in a small running stitch (see Techniques, page 153). When you have finished sewing, pull gently on the running stitch so that the petals form a flower shape.

sew egg cosy Place the egg cosy template on the felt and draw around it twice. Cut out two cosy shapes. Place them together and blanket stitch (see Techniques, page 152) around the curved edges, leaving the straight bottom edge open.

glue on flower Apply felt glue to the back of the flower and press it firmly down on the front of the egg cosy. Do not apply glue to the edges of the petals, as it will prevent them from standing out and creating a 3-D effect.

finishing Apply a dab of glue to the middle of the pompom and stick to the centre of the flower, pressing down firmly. Allow the glue to dry completely.

egg cosies

An ideal gift or just a fun creative craft for the kitchen, these decorative egg cosies are simple to make and look very attractive.

dazzling decorations

flower ice bowl

tissue-paper blooms

fun flowers

paper bells

stained-glass butterflies

star garland

flower ice bowl

Water and fresh flowers are all it takes to make this gorgeous bowl. Fill it with fruit or flowers to make a centrepiece for your party table.

YOU WILL NEED:

2 round bowls, one approximately 2cm/¾in smaller in diameter than the other • jug/pitcher of water • selection of fresh flowers and leaves • weight, such as a stone or can

make first layer   Pour water into a bowl to a depth of 2.5cm/1in. Place it in the freezer until it has frozen solid – this usually takes one or two hours.

add flowers   Once the first layer has frozen, place the smaller bowl inside the larger bowl. Take some clean flowers and leaves and position them in the gap between the two bowls.

make second layer   Once the whole area between the two bowls has been filled with flowers, carefully pour water into the gap until it reaches the edge of the bowls, poking down any flowers that stick out of the top.

finishing   You may find the bowl will start to float, so weigh it down with a stone or can and then place it in the freezer for a few hours. Take it out about 15 minutes before you need it. This will cause it to melt slightly, making it easier to remove the inner and outer bowls.

YOU WILL NEED:
6 sheets of tissue paper per flower • pipe cleaner • scissors • ribbon for hanging

start folding Place the sheets of tissue paper flat on the table in front of you. Starting at the end closest to you, fold the paper concertina-style into folds that are 2cm/¾in wide. Press each fold flat. You could leave the pleated paper under a heavy book overnight to make it as flat as possible, or ask an adult to run a hot iron over the pleats.

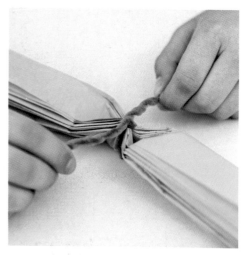

tie paper in middle Mark the centre of the folded paper by folding it in half. Next tie the pipe cleaner around this point and pull it as tightly as you can, gathering the paper together. Twist the ends of the pipe cleaner together and trim the loose ends using scissors. Now tie one end of a length of ribbon around the centre of the folded paper so you can hang up the finished flower.

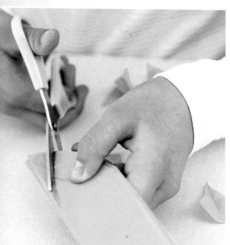

cut ends Make a curved petal shape at the end of each flower by cutting a gentle curve approximately 4cm/1½in in from one end of the tissue paper. Repeat at the other end of the tissue paper.

finishing Gently unfold the pleats of the tissue paper and coax them out into a flower shape. This takes some time and needs to be done very gently and carefully to avoid tearing the delicate paper. Hang the flowers in clusters above the table for your party.

tissue-paper blooms

These giant paper flowers are made from layers of folded tissue paper and are a cheap and easy yet striking decoration for any party or special occasion. Make them in several sizes and hang them from the ceiling using lengths of ribbon.

fun flowers

Layers of coloured card, rick rack trim and buttons are combined to make these vibrant flowers with stems fashioned from drinking straws. Make a group of them to create a striking bouquet in a vase to decorate your house.

YOU WILL NEED:

plain paper • scissors • pencil • pieces of coloured card stock • glue • coloured paper • rick rack trim • decorative buttons • coloured drinking straws • sticky tape

create template Photocopy the templates on page 157 and cut them out. Place a template on the back of a piece of coloured card stock and draw around it in pencil. You need two different colours of card per flower.

cut out flowers Cut out the flowers carefully using scissors. You may find it easier to cut out all the flowers at once and decorate them together. Use scallop-edged scissors or pinking shears for a more decorative effect.

start decorating Stick one flower shape on top of another, making sure that the petals from the lower flower sit between those of the top flower. Now snip circles from coloured paper and stick them onto each flower and petal.

finishing Cut short lengths of rick rack trim and glue to the flower between the centre and each petal. Glue a button to the centre of the flower and one to each petal. Stick the drinking straw stem to the back of the flower using sticky tape, or ask an adult to do this using a hot glue gun.

YOU WILL NEED:

plain paper for template • scissors • pencil • 8 A4/letter-sized pieces decorative paper per bell • glue stick • ribbon • strong/tacky glue • beads • strong thread

create template Photocopy the bell template on page 156 and cut it out using scissors. Place the template on the back of the decorative paper and draw around it using pencil.

cut out bell shapes Use scissors to carefully cut out the bell shape. In total, you will need eight bell shapes for one finished bell, and it's easier to cut out all the shapes in one go.

fold bell shapes Fold each bell in half lengthways, making sure the pretty pattern is on the inside. Glue one half of a bell to one half of the next bell and press flat with your fingers. Continue to glue the bell shapes together, pressing down firmly as you work.

finishing When you reach the last two bell shapes, cut a length of ribbon and stick it to the inside of the top of one side with strong glue. Thread three beads onto thread. Tie a knot in one end of the thread and glue the other end to the inside of the bottom of the bell. Stick the last two sides of the bell together and leave to dry.

paper bells

These decorative paper bells are made
by sticking eight bell shapes together
and look great in pretty pastel designs
but equally good in shades of silver and
gold as festive Christmas decorations.

stained-glass butterflies

These beautiful butterflies make perfect window decorations. Shapes such as butterflies and hearts look great cut from black paper and filled with pieces of brightly coloured tissue paper glued to the back of each shape.

YOU WILL NEED:

plain paper for template •
scissors • pencil • 1 piece
A4/letter-sized black paper
for each shape • white pencil •
coloured tissue paper • PVA/
white glue • black pipe cleaners

create template Photocopy the template on page 157 and cut it out using scissors. Place the template on a piece of black paper then draw round it using the white pencil (to make the butterfly shape easier to see).

cut out butterfly Use the scissors to cut out the butterfly shape from the black paper. If you are making more than one butterfly, it is easier to cut out all the shapes at once before cutting the holes and sticking on the tissue paper.

draw shapes Using the white pencil, draw softly rounded shapes onto the back of the black paper butterfly. Use scissors to carefully cut out these shapes, which form the holes for the tissue paper.

finishing Cut out pieces of tissue paper that are just slightly bigger than the openings and glue to the back of the butterfly shape. Use only a tiny amount of glue, as too much will cause the tissue to get wet and tear. Finish the butterfly with two black pipe-cleaner antennae attached with blobs of glue.

YOU WILL NEED:

paper for template • scissors • pencil • pale and bright pink card stock • sharp thick needle • piece of firm foam (same size as star shape) • PVA/white glue or glue stick • glitter • strong/tacky glue • ribbon

cut out template Photocopy the star template on page 156 and cut it out using scissors. Place it on the back of the card stock and draw round the template with a pencil. Draw around all your stars before you cut them out to save time. You will need six stars of each shade (12 in total) to make the garland.

cut out stars Cut the stars out using scissors. For a more decorative effect, you could use pinking shears or scalloped-edge scissors.

pierce design Place one of the stars onto the piece of firm foam – this makes piercing the holes easier and prevents the card from creasing. Push the needle carefully through the card from the front to back and pull out. Make the next hole approximately 3mm/1⁄8in away from the first, and continue to pierce holes all the way around the edges of the star until finished.

finishing Draw circles in the middle of each star using PVA/white glue. Sprinkle with glitter and leave to dry. To string the garland put a blob of strong/tacky glue on the back of a star point and stick to the ribbon. Continue sticking until the garland is finished.

star garland

Simple card stars cut from bright and paler pink card look
delightful when pierced with a large needle to create a
delicate lacy finish. Decorate the stars with glitter and
string them up on ribbon to create this pretty garland.

cool cards and papercrafts

paper weaving

cheeky crocodile

marbled paper

pressed flower butterfly

stamped gift wrap

pop-up cards

leaf and flower paper

paper weaving

Paper weaving is a simple and effective paper crafting technique. The end result can be used to decorate many items to create attractive and practical gifts (see pages 100–101). You can use odd buttons, self-adhesive dots and pretty rick rack trim to adorn this woven paper mat.

YOU WILL NEED:

4 pieces A4/letter-sized paper in different colours • pencil • ruler • scissors • PVA/white glue • 2 60cm/24in lengths of rick rack braid in different colours • self-adhesive dots • decorative paper • buttons

cut out paper Using a pencil and ruler, draw strips on the back of the different-coloured pieces of paper, making sure that each strip is approximately 2.5cm/1in wide. Using scissors, cut out the strips.

start weaving Lay two different coloured strips of paper at right angles to each other and glue together. Then glue another strip of paper below the top horizontal strip, running parallel to the vertical strip. Now stick a second, horizontal strip to the underside of the vertical strip. Use alternate colour strips and repeat the technique. Weaving the strips under and over each other creates a sturdy mat of woven paper.

continue weaving Continue to weave the strips over and under each other. As you reach the end of the original strips, stick the edge of the strip you are working to either the top or underneath of the original strip and press it down flat. You may need to trim the ends of the strip to make the edges tidy.

finishing When you have stuck down all the ends of the paper strips, decorate the woven paper mat. Stick pretty buttons to each corner on top of a square of polka dot paper. Rick rack trim can be woven through the mat, while self-adhesive dots make a fun finishing touch.

pen pot

A cardboard tube (the sort used to hold potato snacks) can be transformed into a handy pen pot. Cut the pot to the desired height, then decorate it with a piece of woven paper made using the weaving technique. Finish with a pretty band of felt.

handy notebook

Cover a plain notebook with a woven panel and glue on a band of felt braid to make a lovely handmade gift. A piece of card woven with a single strip of paper makes a handy matching bookmark too. Simply cut slits in the card bookmark and weave a paper strip through from front to back. Glue the top and bottom of the strip at the back of the bookmark.

pencil box

Paint a wooden box in a colour that matches one of the paper strips. Measure the lid then weave a panel to fit, to create a simple yet decorative pencil box.

little tips

When covering an item such as a box or front of a notebook, it is better to measure the width and length and divide this measurement equally to make sure the paper strips will fit. If they are between 2–4cm/1–1½in wide, then they will look fine.

YOU WILL NEED:

**plain paper for template ·
scissors · pencil · 1 piece
A4/letter-sized green card
stock (for the large-size
crocodile) · 2 stick-on eyes ·
PVA/white glue · white paint
· fine paintbrush**

create template Photocopy the template on page 156 and cut it out using scissors. Fold the green card stock in half lengthways and place the template on top, lining up the crocodile's spine with the fold of the card, as shown.

snip spiky spine Use scissors to cut out the crocodile. Create the spiky spine effect by marking on the lines as indicated on the template. Snip along the lines through the fold of the card stock. Using a small pair of scissors will keep the cuts neat and tidy.

fold spine Open the crocodile out flat. The cuts will have created six triangular shapes. Fold these back on themselves, pressing them flat with your finger. Carefully fold the crocodile in half again so that the knobbly spines stand up all the way along the crocodile's back.

finishing Glue an eye to each side of the crocodile's face. Using a fine paintbrush, paint on the crocodile's teeth using white paint. You may find it easier to draw the shape of the teeth onto the card in pencil before you paint them.

cheeky crocodile

These fun crocodiles feature knobbly spines, toothy grins and stick-on eyes – make them in different shades of green and an assortment of sizes as decorative additions to your bedroom.

marbled paper

Marbling paper is a very decorative and easy craft, particularly if you use ready-mixed marbling inks, which are available in a good range of colours. Each piece of marbled paper is unique. Use it to cover boxes and notebooks, as well as stationery.

YOU WILL NEED:

marbling inks in different colours • large shallow dish wide enough to hold the paper • stirring stick • A4/letter-sized white paper

add ink Pour about 2.5cm/1in of water into the bowl. Add drops of two or three differently coloured marbling inks to the water. Make sure you only add small amounts of the ink at a time.

stir ink Use a stick to stir the surface of the water. Gently stir the water to create the swirly patterns typical of marbling, taking care not to overmix.

immerse paper Take the sheet of paper and carefully lower it into the bowl so that the whole piece is submerged. Press down lightly with your fingers but be careful not to move the paper around in the bowl.

finishing Carefully lift the paper out of the bowl and allow excess water and ink to run back into the bowl. Place the paper on a flat surface and leave it to dry completely. Use the marbled paper to cover notebooks and finish with a decorative paper initial.

YOU WILL NEED:

white or plain wooden picture frame • white acrylic paint (optional) • paintbrush • pressed flowers, petals, and leaves • glue • plain white paper • scissors

paint frame   If you have a plain wooden frame, paint the outer frame white. Make sure that your brushstrokes follow the direction of the grain of wood. Leave to dry.

add flower petals   When the paint is dry, lay some pressed flowers or petals and leaves on the frame. Play around with the design and when you are happy with it, glue everything in place.

arrange butterfly   Trim a piece of white paper to fit the frame and arrange the remaining flowers and leaves on it in the shape of a butterfly.

finishing   When you are happy with the design, glue the pressed flowers in place. Carefully place the picture in the frame.

pressed flower butterfly

This butterfly picture would make a great decoration for your room or a lovely gift.

stamped gift wrap

It's easy to create your own gift wrap, cards and tags using a rubber stamp and inkpad. We chose a old-fashioned biplane motif which we stamped onto plain white photocopier paper to make this smart gift wrap.

YOU WILL NEED:

rubber stamp with motif of
your choice • ink pad • plain
white photocopier paper •
1 piece of white card stock •
scissors • hole punch • narrow
ribbon for gift tag

apply ink to stamp Hold the
stamp in one hand and dab ink onto the
stamp. Apply enough ink to just cover
the motif.

start stamping Place the stamp in position on the paper
and hold firmly in place but rock the sides gently so that the ink
is transferred evenly over the paper. Continue to stamp at regular
intervals until the paper is covered with the motif.

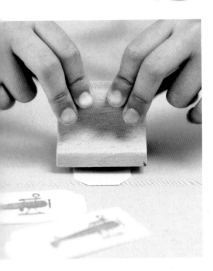

make gift labels Cut out gift tags from white card by cutting a small rectangle
measuring approximately 7 x 4cm/3 x 1½in. Cut the two corners off the top edge at
a 45° angle, then use a hole punch to make a hole in the top. Use the stamp to print
a plane motif in the middle of each tag.

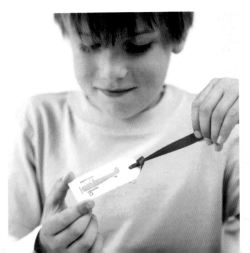

finishing When the ink is dry, thread
the ribbon through the hole in the gift tag
to finish.

YOU WILL NEED:

plain card stock • scissors •
pencil • paper • paints •
paintbrush • rubber/eraser

create template Photocopy
the Christmas tree template on page
156 and cut it out using scissors. Place
the template onto a folded piece of card
stock. Draw around the template in
pencil, lining up the long edge of the
Christmas tree template exactly with
the fold of the paper.

cut out tree shape Using scissors, carefully cut around
the tree shape, making sure you do not cut through the two
sections at the bottom of the tree marked on the template. These
two sections keep the pop-up tree attached to the card itself. If
you find it difficult to cut out the tree, you may wish to ask an adult
to cut it out for you using a craft knife.

fold out design Open out the card carefully and push the Christmas tree shape
forwards so that it stands away from the folded card to create a 3-D effect. Now you
can see how important the uncut side sections are, because they keep the tree shape
attached to the card.

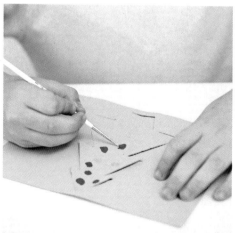

finishing Use a fine paintbrush to draw
spots on the tree to depict decorations.
Add small gift boxes scattered around the
tree to finish the card. You can add glitter
if desired for a more sparkly festive effect.

pop-up cards

These jolly 3-D cards are easy and fun to make and decorate. Try different designs for different occasions. These tree designs are perfect for Christmas, and they also make great thank-you notes for family and friends.

leaf and flower paper

Handmade paper is actually very easy to make. Once you've made one batch, you can make a huge variety of seasonal papers by adding flower petals, leaves and seeds.

YOU WILL NEED:

scrap paper • blender • water • washing-up bowl • embroidery frame • piece of cheesecloth (muslin) or tulle fabric • flat leaves, flowers, and seeds • spoon • towel • hole punch (optional) • ribbon (optional)

make paper pulp Start by making a paper pulp. Tear up some scraps of paper into small pieces and put them in a blender until half full. Pour in enough water so that the blender is three-quarters full. Ask an adult to help you to whizz the mixture until you have a pulp.

add water Pour the paper pulp into a large bowl, such as a washing-up bowl. Add 2 jugs/pitchers of water, approximately 2 litres/3½ pints, and mix it all around with your hands. It's very messy!

cut fabric Separate the two sections of the embroidery frame. Lay a piece of fine fabric, such as cheesecloth (muslin) or tulle, over the smaller section and measure and cut a square approximately 3cm/1¼in larger than the frame.

attach frame Place the larger section of the embroidery frame over the smaller and tighten. Try not to push the two sections together so that they are level with each other, but leave the outer frame slightly raised above the smaller one.

dip frame Now for the fun bit! Swish your hands around in the water so that the pulp is evenly distributed. Dip the frame down away from you and lower it into the water at an angle. Straighten it up under the water and then slowly bring it out. Let the water drip through.

position leaves Rest the frame on the side of the bowl and position your leaves, flowers, or seeds on top. Pour some of the pulp mixture over the flowers and leaves using a spoon.

remove frame Gently place the frame on a towel, remove the frame, and let dry for several hours or overnight. The next day it should be dry and you can carefully peel the paper away from the fabric.

finishing To make a notebook, cut out some rectangles from the paper circle to make a front and back cover. Cut some plain paper the same size for the inside of the book. Punch holes through all the layers, thread some ribbon through, and tie together.

funky fashions

fleece scarf

fleece hat

elasticated skirt

PJ shorts

guitar t-shirt

heart t-shirt

decorated jeans

fleece scarf

This cosy scarf decorated with pretty flowers is made from soft fleece fabric that does not require hemming as it doesn't fray, making it the ideal fabric for this project.

YOU WILL NEED:
20cm x 1m/8in x 3ft piece of fleece fabric • scissors • paper • 2 or 3 squares of coloured felt for flowers • scraps of coloured felt for flower centres • fusible web • pins • needle • 3 buttons (2cm/¾in diameter) • contrasting embroidery thread

cut fabric and fringe Take the piece of fleece and along the two shorter edges, cut slits about 2cm/¾in apart to create the fringing.

create template Photocopy the flower and circle template on page 155 and cut it out with scissors. Ask an adult to help you iron the fusible web onto the back of the felt for the flowers and allow the fabric to cool. Place the flower template on the paper side of the fusible web and draw around it six times. Cut out the flower shapes.

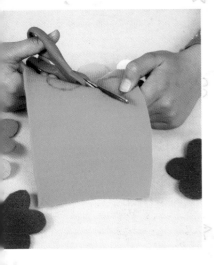

cut out flowers Now place the circle template on the paper side of the remaining felt scraps, draw around it and cut out six circle shapes.

finishing Peel off the backing paper and position three flowers at each end of the scarf. Ask an adult to help you iron them in place, following the manufacturer's instructions. Using embroidery thread, blanket stitch (see Techniques, page 152) around the flowers. Stitch a felt circle and button to the middle of each flower to finish.

YOU WILL NEED:

paper • scissors • pins • 30cm/12in fleece fabric (137cm/54in wide) • 3 or 4 squares different-coloured felt for flower and leaves • fusible web • 1 button (2cm/⅜in diameter) • contrast embroidery thread • standard needle • large needle • double knitting wool

create templates Photocopy the hat, leaf, circle and flowers templates on page 155 and cut them out. Fold the fleece fabric in two, pin the hat template to the fabric and cut out two shapes. Now ask an adult to help you iron the fusible web to the squares of felt. Place the flower and leaf templates on the paper side of the fusible web and draw around them. You will need two leaves, one flower and one circle. Cut out the shapes. Peel off the backing fabric and ask an adult to help you iron the motifs to the front of the hat.

add decoration Work blanket stitch (see Techniques, page 152) all the way around the flower and leaf shapes and then firmly sew a felt circle and a button to the middle of the flower.

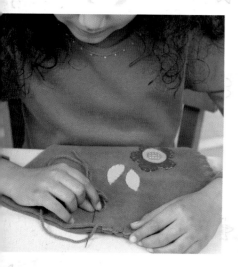

stitch hat Lay the two hat sections together with wrong sides facing and stitch all the way around the curved edges using blanket stitch and knitting wool.

finishing Work blanket stitch along the bottom straight edge of the hat on the inside. Make a turning to the outside of the hat approximately 3cm/1¼in to create a fold and secure it in place with a couple of stitches on both sides of the hat.

fleece hat

Make this cute matching hat to wear with your scarf – it's finished with a felt flower and leaves and edged in wool blanket stitch.

elasticated skirt

This pretty skirt is made from a cotton fabric gathered with elastic and adorned with fun appliquéd fabric flowers decorated with blanket stitch and finished with buttons.

YOU WILL NEED:

35cm x 1m/14in x 3ft cotton fabric • pinking shears • scraps of fabric for flowers • fusible web • paper • scissors • pencil • embroidery thread • needle • sewing thread • 3 buttons (1cm/½in diameter) • 60cm/24in elastic (2.5cm/1in wide) • 20cm/8in ribbon (2cm/¾in wide) • safety pin

cut out skirt For the skirt, cut two pieces of fabric each measuring 35 x 85cm/14 x 34in, using pinking shears to prevent the fabric edges from fraying. Place the two pieces together with right sides facing and stitch along one short end using back stitch (see Techniques, page 153) and working 1cm/½in from the raw edge.

create template Ask an adult to help you iron the fusible web to the back of the flower fabric and let it cool. Photocopy the flower template on page 155 and cut it out. Place the template on the paper side of the fusible web and draw around it three times to create three flower motifs. Peel off the backing paper and position the three flowers on the front of the skirt fabric. Ask an adult to help you iron them in place following the manufacturer's instructions and allow to cool.

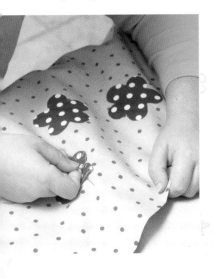

stitch round on flowers Thread the needle with the embroidery thread and work blanket stitch (see Techniques, page 152) all the way around the flower motifs.

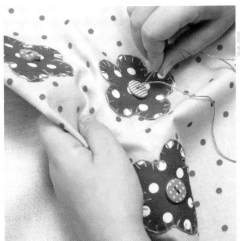

sew on buttons Once you have worked blanket stitch around all three of the flowers, sew a button to the middle of each flower. Make sure you cast off carefully so that the buttons are secure.

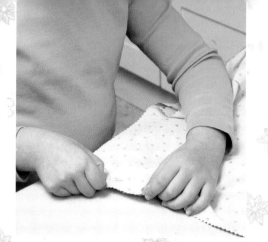

stitch side seams Fold the skirt fabric together with right sides facing. Use back stitch (see Techniques, page 153) to stitch together the short ends, working 1cm/½in from the raw edges. Notch the seam so it lies flat and ask an adult to help you to press open the seam using a hot iron.

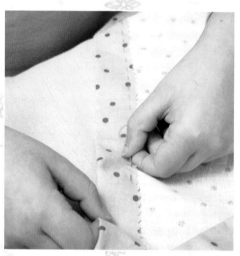

sew hem and elastic casing Fold over the top and bottom edges of the fabric by 3cm/1¼in to form a hem at the bottom and a casing for the elastic at the top. Sew in place using small running stitches (see Techniques, page 153). Leave the ends of the casing open so you can insert the elastic.

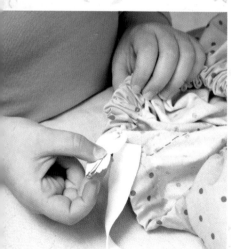

insert elastic Wrap the elastic around your waist until you find a length that feels comfortable. Cut the elastic to this length then attach the safety pin to one end. Insert the elastic into the casing through one opening. Chase the elastic all the way through the casing and out the other end. Remove the safety pin and securely stitch together the two ends of the elastic.

finishing Sew the elastic casing opening closed using whipstitch (see Techniques, page 153). Tie the ribbon in a bow and trim the ribbon ends on the diagonal to prevent them from fraying. Stitch the bow to the front of the waistband to finish.

PJ shorts

Make these cute shorts from old
pyjama bottoms and trim them with
colourful rick rack and a ribbon bow.

YOU WILL NEED:
1 pair old pyjamas • scissors
• pins • needle • sewing thread
• 1.2m/4ft rick rack

trim legs Cut the legs off the pyjama bottoms about 5cm/2in down from the crotch. Use sharp scissors and cut a curved shape at the outside of each leg.

hem edges On the first leg, turn up a double hem to hide the raw edge and pin it in place if necessary. Repeat with the second leg. Sew the hems in place using whipstitch (see Techniques, page 153), then ask an adult to help you press them flat using a hot iron. Allow the fabric to cool.

sew on trim Cut a length of rick rack and use running stitch (see Techniques, page 153), to stitch it around the first leg, about 5mm/¼in up from the bottom. When you have finished, fold the raw edge of the rick rack to the inside and finish with small whipstitches (see Techniques, page 153) to secure. Repeat on the other leg.

finishing Cut a length of rick rack measuring approximately 20cm/8in. Tie it into a bow and cut the ends on the diagonal to prevent them from fraying. Stitch the bow to the centre of the waistband to finish.

YOU WILL NEED:

30 x 30cm/12 x 12in star-print fabric for guitar motif
• 30 x 30cm/12 x 12in fusible web • paper • pencil • scissors
• plain long-sleeved t-shirt
• contrasting coloured embroidery thread • 3 assorted buttons • sewing thread
• 3-D fabric paint

create template

Ask an adult to help you iron the fusible web to the back of the star fabric and let it cool. Photocopy the template on page 154 and cut it out. Place the template on the paper side of the fusible web, draw around it and cut out the guitar shape. Peel off the backing paper and position the guitar in place on the front of the t-shirt. Ask an adult to help you iron it in place, following the manufacturer's instructions, and allow to cool.

stitch around motif

Thread the needle with the embroidery thread and begin stitching all the way around the guitar motif in blanket stitch (see Techniques, page 152).

sew on buttons

Stitch the three buttons on to the guitar using sewing thread. Make sure you cast off your sewing securely, so it does not come undone.

finishing

Use the 3-D fabric pen to draw tiny dots along the handle of the guitar. Allow the paint to dry completely before wearing the t-shirt.

guitar t-shirt

Customize a plain t-shirt with this cool electric guitar motif decorated with blanket stitch and colourful buttons.

heart t-shirt

A simple heart-shaped motif in floral
fabric is decorated with tiny coloured
buttons to create this pretty t-shirt.

YOU WILL NEED:
20 x 20cm/8 x 8in floral fabric for heart motif • 20 x 20cm/ 8 x 8in fusible web • plain long-sleeved t-shirt • scissors • pencil • contrasting coloured embroidery thread • needle • sewing thread • 5 small buttons

create template Ask an adult to help you iron the fusible web to the back of the floral fabric and allow to cool. Photocopy the heart template on page 154 and cut out with scissors. Place the template on the paper side of the fusible web and draw around it in pencil.

cut out heart shape Cut out the heart. Peel off the backing paper and position it in place on the front of the t-shirt. Ask an adult to help you iron it in place, following the manufacturer's instructions, and allow to cool.

stitch around motif Thread the needle with the embroidery thread and begin stitching all the way around the heart motif in blanket stitch (see Techniques, page 152). When you finish, cast off securely to prevent the stitching from coming undone.

finishing Use the sewing thread to sew the five buttons to the heart. Make sure you cast off your sewing securely, so it does not come undone.

YOU WILL NEED:
pair of plain blue jeans (this project works best with bootcut jeans) • 1m/3ft rick rack • 1m/3ft rick rack in a different colour • sewing thread • needle • 60 small beads • 60 small buttons • fine needle for beads • scissors

stitch rick rack   Cut a length of rick rack to fit around the bottom of the first leg. Use running stitch (see Techniques, page 153) to sew it in place, stitching about 2.5cm/1in up from the hem. Trim the end of the rick rack, fold the raw edge inside and use whipstitch (see Techniques, page 153) to secure in place. Repeat with the other leg.

sew on beads   Starting with the first leg, use a fine needle to sew the tiny beads all along the rick rack at 1cm/½in intervals. Repeat on the second leg.

attach more rick rack   Use running stitch to attach a second row of rick rack braid all the way around the bottom of the first leg, sewing it in place about 2cm/¾in above the first row. Trim the end of the rick rack, fold the raw edge to the inside and use slipstitch to secure it in place.

finishing   Working on the first leg, stitch the tiny buttons in a row at 1cm/½in intervals, sewing them about 2cm/¾in up from the rick rack. Make sure you cast off the stitching securely when you have finished. Repeat on the second leg of the jeans to finish.

decorated jeans

Update a plain pair of jeans with rows of colourful rick rack, tiny beads and colourful buttons to give them instant appeal. This would work equally well on plain coloured trousers too.

awesome accessories

handy shopper

bead necklace

duffel bag

felt tool wrap

star headband

handy shopper

This useful shopping bag makes a great gift for a mother or a grandparent. Made from cream calico, it is stencilled with a cheerful boat motif and trimmed with lengths of colourful rick rack. You could also stencil on your initials to personalize the bag.

YOU WILL NEED:

2 pieces of calico each measuring 52 x 40cm/21 x 16in • pinking shears • 80cm/32in red rick rack • 80cm/32in green rick rack • needle • thread • boat stencil • red and blue fabric paint • stencil brush • masking tape • embroidery thread • 80cm/32in cream cotton ribbon for handles • 80cm/32in jumbo rick rack

cut out fabric Take the two pieces of fabric measuring 52 x 40cm/21 x 16in and trim the edges using pinking shears to prevent them from fraying.

sew on rick rack Cut the two lengths of rick rack in half, so you have four lengths in total. Take one of the pieces of calico. This will be the front of the bag. Pin a length of rick rack across the calico, parallel to one of the shorter edges and about 5cm/2in in from the edge of the fabric. Stitch the rick rack in place using running stitch (see Techniques, page 153). Next, pin then stitch the second row of rick rack in place about 3cm/1¼in above this. Repeat at the other end of the fabric, stitching the first row of rick rack about 8cm/3in in from the raw edge and the second row about 3cm/1¼in above the first.

stencil design on bag Place the stencil in the centre of the front fabric piece, spaced evenly between the rows of rick rack. Use masking tape to hold the corners in place. Dip the stencil brush in the fabric paint and blot any excess paint on a piece of kitchen paper so that the brush is fairly dry. Fill in the waves motif with blue paint, using a dabbing motion. Leave the paint to dry completely.

remove stencil When the blue paint is completely dry, cover it with masking tape. Now use the red fabric paint to fill in the rest of the stencil detail. Leave to dry. When the paint is completely dry, carefully peel off the stencil to reveal the motif.

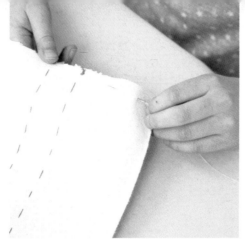

stitch bag together Pin the two pieces of calico together with right sides facing, so the stencil and rick rack trim are on the inside. Stitch the two long sides and one short side of the bag together using back stitch (see Techniques, page 153) and strong sewing thread. Leave the top edge of the bag open.

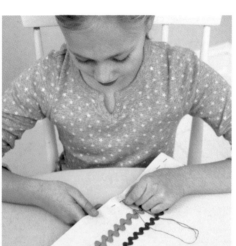

sew top hem Fold 3cm/1¼in of the top edge of the bag to the inside and ask an adult to help you press the hem flat using a hot iron. Stitch the hem in place using running stitch and contrasting coloured embroidery thread for a decorative effect.

make handles Lay a row of jumbo rick rack along the centre of each 40cm/16in piece of handle and pin it in place. Stitch the rick rack to the first handle piece using running stitch. Repeat for the second handle.

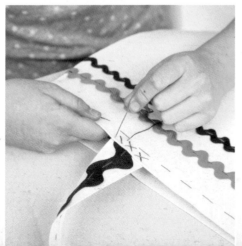

finishing Stitch the handles to the front and back of the bag about 12cm/5in in from the side seams and use three large cross stitches to hold them securely in place. You may wish to make the handles stronger by stitching around them on the inside using whipstitch (see Techniques, page 153) and cream sewing thread.

bead
necklace

A combination of felt and
wooden beads and felt
flowers have been used
to create this delightful
necklace finished with
a dainty velvet bow.

YOU WILL NEED:

strong thread for threading
• 1 small wooden bead • large
needle for threading • 35
wooden beads • 9 felt flowers
• 5 felt beads • scissors •
15cm/6in narrow velvet ribbon

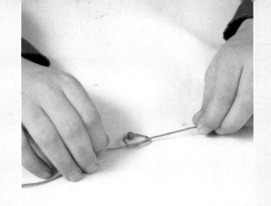

knot end of thread String the small wooden bead onto the thread and tie in a knot at one end. This will prevent the beads from slipping off the end of the thread while you are stringing them.

thread beads Push the other end of the thread through the needle. Thread five of the wooden beads in assorted colours onto the necklace. It helps to have all the beads in front of you while you work, so you can choose which colour to thread onto the necklace next.

continue threading When you have added five wooden beads, thread a felt flower then a felt bead followed by another felt flower. Then thread another five wooden beads followed by a single felt flower. Now add another five wooden beads followed by a felt flower, bead and flower, and repeat until you have strung on all the beads and flowers. Leave approximately 8cm/3in of thread free at the end for tying the necklace.

finishing Tie the ends of the thread together in several strong knots then trim the ends with scissors. Tie the ribbon around the necklace and finish it in a bow. Trim the ribbon ends on the diagonal to prevent them from fraying.

YOU WILL NEED:

25 x 25 cm/10 x 10in red fabric
• needle • embroidery thread •
20 x 20cm/8 x 8in gingham
fabric • fusible web • paper •
pencil • scissors • 1m/3ft fabric
(137cm/54in wide) for main
bag • pins • 1.4m/4½ft cotton
cord • 6cm/2½in gingham
ribbon (2cm/¾in wide)
• safety pin

make pocket Take the square of red fabric for the pocket. Fold the four edges 1cm/½in to the inside and ask an adult to help you press them flat with a hot iron. Allow the fabric to cool then sew along one edge using running stitch (see Techniques, page 153). This will be the top, open edge of the pocket.

stitch initial to pocket Iron the fusible web to the back of the piece of gingham fabric. Draw your chosen initial on a piece of paper then cut it out to use as a template. Place the initial template on the paper side of the fusible web and draw around it (remember that you will need to reverse non-symmetrical initials when drawing them on the back of fabric). Cut out the initial. Peel off the backing paper and position it in the middle of the pocket. Ask an adult to help you iron it in place, following the manufacturer's instructions, and allow to cool. Now work blanket stitch (see Techniques, page 152) all the way around the initial.

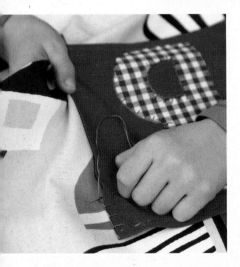

sew on pocket Cut a piece of fabric measuring 60cm/2ft in length. This will form the body of the duffle bag. Pin the pocket to the centre front of the fabric then sew it in place using blanket stitch.

sew side seam Fold the piece of fabric in half with the right sides facing. Pin if necessary then stitch all the way along the long edge using back stitch (see Techniques, page 153) and working 1cm/½in from the raw edge. Leave a 2.5cm/1in opening about 6cm/2½in down from one end of the fabric – this is where you will insert the drawstring cord.

duffel bag

This handy duffel bag is useful for holidays, to hold swimming kit or as an overnight bag for sleepovers!

sew base to bag Cut out a circle of 22cm/9in diameter from the bag fabric. This is the base of the bag. Place the circle on the bottom of the bag, right side facing in. Fold the gingham ribbon in two to form a loop, then insert it between the bottom of the bag and the bottom piece, making sure the loop is facing towards the inside of the bag and the ends are between the two pieces of fabric. Stitch the base to the bag using back stitch.

make casing for cord Turn the top edge of the bag 3cm/1¼in to the inside and ask an adult to help you press it flat with a hot iron. Allow the fabric to cool then turn the bag right side out and stitch the top seam in place using running stitch (see Techniques, page 153). Leave the sides of the seam open so you can insert the drawstring cord.

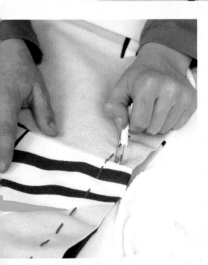

insert the cord Wrap a small piece of sticky tape around one end of the cord to prevent it from fraying and attach the safety pin to this end. Insert the cord into the casing through one of the open ends of the seam at the top of the bag. Use the safety pin to chase the cord all the way through the casing and out through the other end.

finishing Remove the safety pin and thread one end of the cord through the gingham ribbon loop. Now tie the cord ends together in a secure knot. Trim the ends of the cord, leaving approximately 2cm/¾in at each end. Fray the ends of the cord by hand.

YOU WILL NEED:

paper • scissors • 1 piece red felt 43 x 30cm/17 x 12in • 1 piece blue felt 43 x 30cm/ 17 x 12in • 1 smaller piece red felt 43 x 15cm/17 x 6in • 20 x 20cm/8 x 8in gingham • fusible web • pencil • contrasting coloured embroidery thread • pinking shears • 60cm/24in gingham ribbon (2cm/¾in wide)

create template Photocopy the slanted pocket template on page 155 and cut out. Then cut out two pieces of felt measuring 43 x 30cm/17 x 12in, one from blue felt and one from red felt. Pin the pocket template on to the smaller 43 x 15cm/17 x 6in piece of red felt and cut all the way around it.

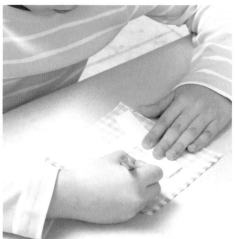

create initial Iron the fusible web to the back of the gingham fabric and leave it to cool. Draw your chosen initial on a piece of paper then cut it out to use as a template. Place the initial template on the paper side of the fusible web and draw all the way around it. Remember that you will need to reverse non-symmetrical initials when drawing them on the back of fabric.

cut out initial Carefully cut out the initial. Peel off the backing paper and position it on the front of the larger red felt rectangle in the front bottom corner. This will be the front of the tool wrap. Ask an adult to help you use a hot iron to fix in place, following the manufacturer's instructions. Let it cool.

start blanket stitch Thread a needle with embroidery thread and work blanket stitch (see Techniques, page 152) all the way around the initial. The stitches should be about 5mm/¼in apart. Cast off securely when you have finished.

felt tool wrap

A great gift for Father's Day, this colourful
and practical felt tool wrap features an appliquéd
gingham initial and gingham ribbon ties. You could
also make it in a strong fabric such as denim – try
using the bottom of an old pair of adult jeans.

stitch sections Place the blue felt fabric on a flat surface. Place the red pocket section on top, lining up the bottom and side edges. Pin in position if required. Now stitch six lines of running stitch at regularly spaced intervals to attach the pocket to the felt. These will create seven pockets for the tools.

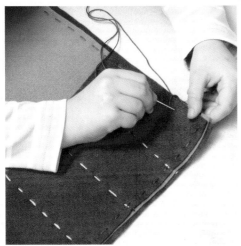

stitch layers together Next lay the blue fabric plus pocket on top of the main red fabric section with wrong sides of the fabric facing and use running stitch (see Techniques, page 153) to sew around all four edges, stitching approximately 1cm/½in from the edge of the felt.

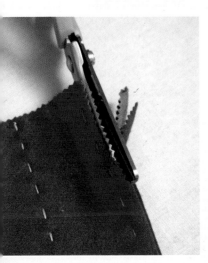

trim edges When you have finished sewing the felt together, use pinking shears to trim all four edges of the fabric for a decorative effect. Be careful not to cut through any of your stitching.

finishing Measure 20cm/8in in from the end of the ribbon and make a fold. Stitch the fold to the front of the tool wrap on the inside using whipstitch (see Techniques, page 153). The ribbon should be positioned about halfway between the top and bottom of the wrap.

YOU WILL NEED:

strips of thick decorated paper (measuring 20 x 2cm/8 x 1in for largest star) • headband • strong/tacky glue

form knot shape Make a knot approximately a third of the way along one strip of paper. Pull as firmly as you can without the paper tearing and press the knot flat between your fingers to form a five-sided pentagon, with the two long paper ends sticking out from two of the five sides.

fold paper Fold the shorter end of the paper across the pentagon shape and press flat with your finger. Tuck the end of the paper inside the fold created by the knot on the inside of the pentagon shape.

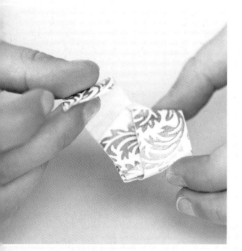

continue folding Fold the remaining longer length of paper over the pentagon shape, following the shape of the pentagon. Fold the end of the paper inside the pentagon shape to finish.

finishing Use your thumbnail to gently push in the flat folded edges of the pentagon shape and to gently coax the shape into becoming a more 3–D star shape. Try blowing gently inside the star to further inflate the shape and to puff it up more. Make a selection of different-sized stars and use glue to stick them to the headband.

star headband

This pretty headband is decorated with delicate paper stars made by folding lengths of narrow paper. We used a selection of different-sized stars which were then stuck onto a headband.

blanket stitch

Blanket stitch is usually worked in wool to finish the raw edges of a blanket or wool fabrics. It is a pretty, decorative stitch that is useful for creating a bold outline. Use tapestry or knitting yarn for this stitch.

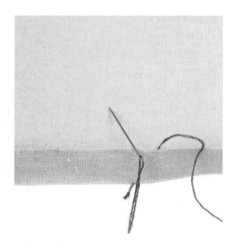 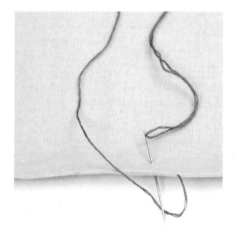 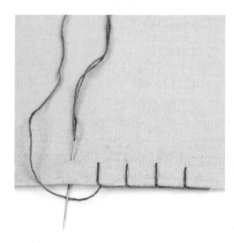

1 Fold up the raw edges of the fabric approximately 1cm/½in to the inside. Press in place if necessary. Now push the needle through the fabric from the wrong side so it emerges from the folded crease. Carefully pull the needle all the way through.

2 Next, push the needle through the front of the fabric, about 1cm/½in along from the previous stitch or at the distance stated in the step by step instructions. Pull the needle out through the fold of the hem with the thread looped underneath the point of the needle. Pull the thread through.

3 Repeat the stitch, always remembering to loop the thread under the point of the needle to create the blanket stitch. Take care not to pull the thread too tight. Always keep the stitches evenly spaced – it is best not to work them too far apart.

running stitch, back stitch and whipstitch

These simple but essential stitches are all very easy to master. Try practising them on scraps of fabric before starting a project.

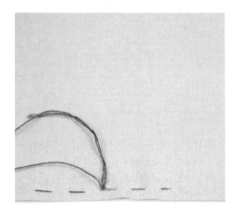 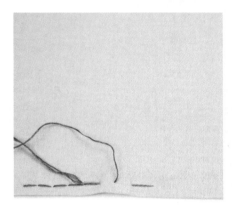 

Running stitch This is a series of small, straight stitches that are equal in length on both sides of the fabric. Thread the needle and work from the edge of the fabric pushing the needle through the fabric from front to back and then pushing the needle back through to the front of the fabric again.

Back stitch Thread the needle and work from the edge of the fabric – push the needle through from the back of the fabric to the front. Rather than pushing the needle in front, put it back behind where it was to create a stitch approximately 8–10mm wide. Repeat by pushing the needle back through the fabric as you work the stitch to create a neat line of stitches that resemble a line of sewing machine stitches with no gaps.

Whipstitch This stitch is for neatly sewing openings closed and joining together two layers of fabric. Work on the wrong side of the fabric. Start with a knot and the needle in the fold. Push the needle through the two layers from back to front and pull the thread through. Insert the needle into the hem again and make another stitch about 5mm/¼in from the first. Continue making stitches and cast off with a few close stitches.

templates

The outlines shown on pages 154–157 have
been reduced in size so they fit on these
pages. Before cutting out the templates,
you must enlarge them on a photocopier by
200 per cent to make them the right size.

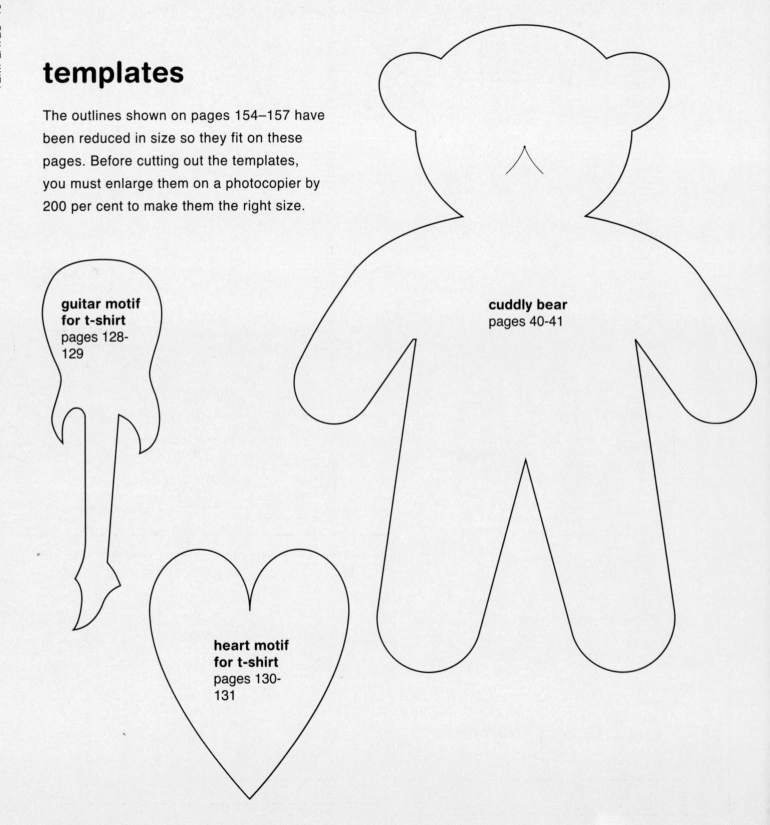

**guitar motif
for t-shirt**
pages 128-
129

cuddly bear
pages 40-41

**heart motif
for t-shirt**
pages 130-
131

pocket for tool wrap
pages 146-149

fleece hat
pages 120-121

leaf for hat
pages 120-121

flower for hat and scarf
pages 118-121

flower for elasticated skirt
pages 122-125

flower centre for hat and scarf
pages 118-121

playing piece for travel game
pages 16-19

Finger puppet
pages 38-39

house for appliqué cushion
pages 68-71

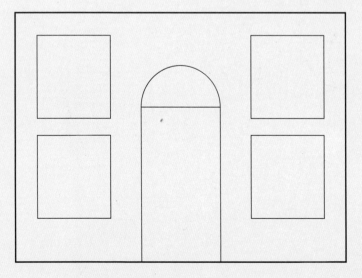

egg cosy
pages 80-81

flower petal for egg cosy

templates

The outlines shown on pages 154–157 have been reduced in size so they fit on these pages. Before cutting out the templates, you must enlarge them on a photocopier by 200 per cent to make them the right size.

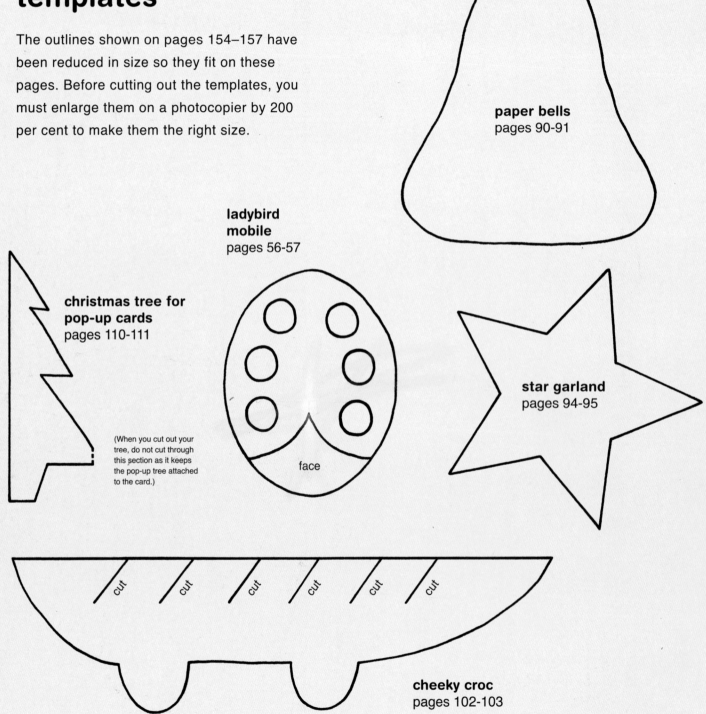

paper bells
pages 90-91

ladybird mobile
pages 56-57

christmas tree for pop-up cards
pages 110-111

(When you cut out your tree, do not cut through this section as it keeps the pop-up tree attached to the card.)

face

star garland
pages 94-95

cut cut cut cut cut cut

cheeky croc
pages 102-103

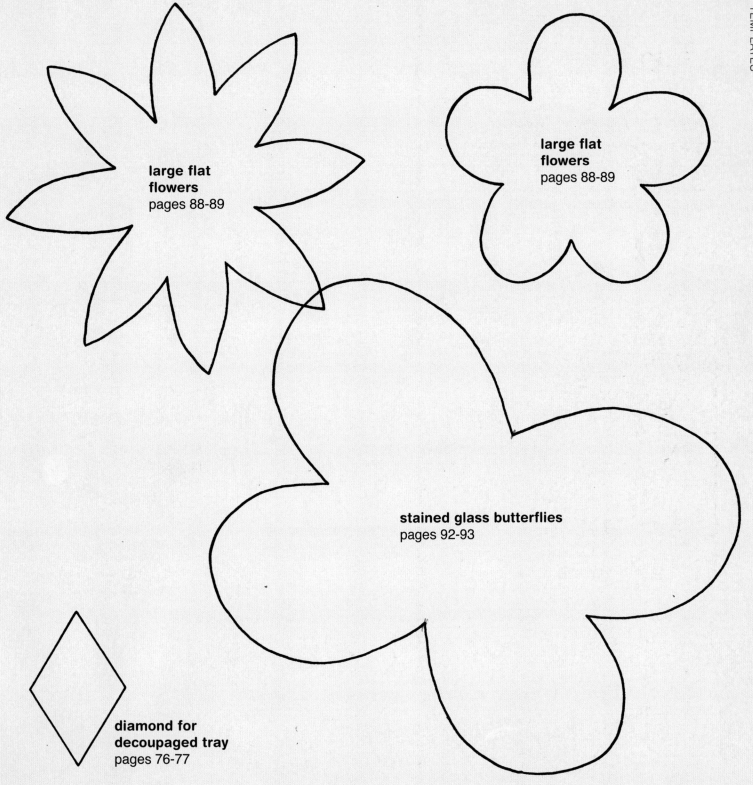

large flat flowers
pages 88-89

large flat flowers
pages 88-89

stained glass butterflies
pages 92-93

diamond for decoupaged tray
pages 76-77

UK sources

BEADWORKS BEAD SHOP
21a Tower Street
London WC2H 9NS
0207 240 0931
www.beadworks.co.uk

*Glass beads, pearls, rocailles
and bugle beads plus
findings and jewellery tools.*

THE BUTTON QUEEN
76 Marylebone Lane
London W1U 2PR
0207 935 1505
www.thebuttonqueen.co.uk

*Buttons from pearl and wood
to colourful plastic. They also
offer a button-covering service
in a wide range of designs
using your own fabric.*

CALICO CRAFTS
www.calicocrafts.co.uk

*Online crafts specialist with
large haberdashery section
and useful fabrics including
calico and gingham.*

CALICO LAINE
0151 336 3939
www.calicolaine.co.uk

*Fleece fabric, felt, trims,
coloured elastic, braid,*

*fusible web, stick-on eyes,
gingham, craft materials,
embellishments and general
haberdashery.*

**CREATIONS ART AND
CRAFT MATERIALS**
01326 555777
www.ecreations.co.uk

*Online craft store with large
stock of buttons, decorative
fabric motifs, cord, ribbon
and elastic, and fabric paints
as well as all the usual
sewing accessories.*

**THE ENGLISH STAMP
COMPANY**
01929 439117
www.englishstamp.com

*Rubber stamps that can also
be customized to include
your child's name or address.
From simple designs to more
complex motifs, the selection
is comprehensive and
available in different sizes.
Also stocks a good selection
of coloured stamping inks.*

HOBBYCRAFT
Westway Cross Shopping Park
Greenford Road
London UB6 0UW
0845 0516528
www.hobbycraft.co.uk

*Chain of craft superstores
carrying embroidery thread,
sewing accessories, ribbons,
haberdashery, fusible web
and a wide selection of
decorative buttons.*

HOMECRAFTS DIRECT
0116 269 7733
www.homecrafts.co.uk

*Sewing motifs, fancy threads,
ribbon and braid, fancy trims,
glass, wooden and plastic
beads and brooch backs as
well as fleece fabrics and felt.*

IKEA
Visit www.ikea.co.uk for a
catalogue or details of your
nearest store.

*Wooden boxes and files and
plain picture frames for
decorating or decoupaging
as well as a good selection of
furnishing fabrics.*

JOHN LEWIS
Visit www.johnlewis.com for
details of your nearest store.

*The store's haberdashery
department stocks a good*

range of buttons, rick rack and ribbon plus all the usual sewing accessories.

SEWING AND CRAFT SUPERSTORE

296–312 Balham High Road
London SW17 7AA
0208 767 0036
www.craftysewer.com

Everything from beads and sequins to fusible web, brooch backs, polyester toy stuffing, stick-on eyes and beaded motifs.

THE STENCIL LIBRARY

Stocksfield Hall
Northumberland NE43 7TN
www.stencil-library.com

Great selection of stencils from simple designs to large complex motifs. They also supply a good range of fabric paints and brushes.

VV ROULEAUX

261 Pavillion Road
London SW1X 0PB
0207 730 3125
www.vvrouleaux.com

Ribbons, rick rack and braids in silk, cotton and velvet plus embroidered motifs and fabric flowers.

US sources

A.C. MOORE

Call 866-342-8802 or visit www.acmoore.com for your nearest store.

Craft superstores carrying polyester toy stuffing, notions, ribbons, sewing supplies, embroidery thread, stencils, wooden clothespins, and embroidery hoops.

BRITEX FABRICS

146 Geary Street
San Francisco, CA 94108
415-392-2910
www.britexfabrics.com

Ribbons, décor trims and tassels, and notions.

THE BUTTON EMPORIUM & RIBBONRY

1016 SW Taylor Street
Portland, OR 97205
503-228-6372
www.buttonemporium.com

Vintage and assorted decorative buttons.

HEART OF THE HOME STENCILS

www.stencils4u.com
888–675–1695

Alphabet stencils as well as other simple designs for kids.

HOBBY LOBBY

Visit www.hobbylobby.com for your nearest store.

Fleece and calico fabrics as well as children's prints. Also sewing supplies, notions, ribbons, trims and buttons.

HYMAN HENDLER & SONS

21 West 38th Street
New York, NY 10018
212-840-8393
www.hymanhendler.com

Novelty and vintage ribbons.

IKEA

Visit www.ikea.com/us for your nearest store.

Unpainted wooden photo frames, plain tins for découpaging, and cute accessories.

JO-ANN FABRICS

Locations nationwide. Visit www.joann.com for your nearest store.

A wide selection of sewing supplies.

KARI ME AWAY

www.karimeaway.com

Rick rack and bobble trims in a large variety of colours. Also novelty buttons and glass beads.

MICHAELS

Visit www.michaels.com for your nearest store.

Every kind of fabric craft material, including beads, fabric paints, embroidery thread, yarns, glues, and elastic.

M&J TRIMMING

www.mjtrim.com

Fancy trims, including rhinestones, sequined flowers, ribbons, lace, rosettes, beaded braid, and fur and feather trims.

THE RIBBONERIE

3695 Sacramento Street
San Francisco, CA 94118
415-626-6184
www.ribbonerie.com

Extensive collection including wired, grosgrain, metallic, and velvet ribbons.

TINSEL TRADING CO.

1 West 37th Street
New York, NY 10018
212-730-1030
www.tinseltrading.com

Vintage buttons and beads, as well as gorgeous silk and velvet flowers, sequins, metallic tassels, and exquisite ribbons.

index

credits

All projects by Catherine Woram
except for those on pages 20–21,
24–25, 44–45, 50–51, 62–63,
84–85, 106–107 and 112–115
by Clare Youngs.

Photography credits

Claire Richardson
20–21,24–25, 44–45, 50–51,
62–63, 84–85,106–107, 112–115

Penny Wincer
16–19, 30–31, 38–39, 40–43,
48–49, 52–55, 58–59, 66–67,
68–71, 74–75, 80–81, 118–119,
120–121, 122–125, 126–127,
128–129, 130–131, 132–133,
136–139, 140–141, 142–145,
146–149

Polly Wreford
10–11, 12–13, 14–15, 22–23,
26–27, 32–33, 34–37, 56–57,
60–61, 72–74, 76–77, 78–79,
86–87, 88–89, 90–91, 92–93,
94–95, 98–101, 102–103,
104–105, 108–109, 110–111,
150–151